THE BACKYARD BIRDING BIBLE

5 in 1

How to Attract, Record, Identify and Photograph Birds in
Your Garden | Including DIY Bird Houses, Feeders, and Baths

Rowan T. Wiedemann

TABLE OF CONTENTS

INTRODUCTION

For centuries, birds have captivated humans with their beauty, fascinating behaviors, and melodious songs. Watching birds connects us to nature and provides a peaceful respite from our busy lives. The hobby of birdwatching has exploded in popularity in recent years as more people discover the joys of observing backyard birds. This book provides everything you need to fully engage with the avian world right outside your window.

The Backyard Birding Bible is the ultimate five-in-one guide to transforming your outdoor space into a birdwatcher's paradise that attracts a diversity of species and enables you to fully enjoy garden birds through observation, identification, recording, photography, and hands-on projects. The book begins by exploring how to convert your yard into an ideal bird habitat. You'll discover optimal plants, flowers, trees, and water features to entice birds using their natural food sources and cover. You'll also learn specialized techniques for providing bird feeders and baths to meet birds' daily needs while deterring predators. With the right habitat enrichments, your backyard will soon host a lively menagerie of colorful songbirds all year round.

The book next dives into the vital skill of systematic bird observation and recording. You'll set up a daily birding journal using both analog and digital tools for comprehensively documenting the bird species visiting your yard. Recording detailed notes and analyzing patterns over time provides valuable insights into bird behaviors and seasonal movements. The book shares tips for when during the day different species tend to be most active at feeders and how weather impacts backyard bird populations. These observation techniques allow you to intimately connect with individual birds.

At the heart of the book is a complete education in bird identification. You'll learn how to recognize birds by sight and sound. We explore the anatomy and plumage characteristics that distinguish species as well as the unique songs and calls of backyard birds. Understanding migration patterns and cycles is key to identifying seasonal populations in your area. You'll discover how to master reputable field guides and make quick annotations for confirming identifications. With knowledge and practice, you'll be ready to confidently identify every flutter and tweet in your garden.

Arguably, the most exciting aspect of backyard birding is photographing your avian visitors. This book reveals expert techniques for capturing professional-quality bird images right in your yard. You'll learn how to select the optimal camera equipment and settings for clear, vivid photographs that showcase fine details. Tips are provided for photographing birds in flight, optimal lighting and compositional strategies, and using backgrounds creatively. You'll discover how to focus quickly when action strikes and get eye-level portraits. The book also covers post-processing methods for perfecting your images.

To fully immerse yourself in the birding lifestyle, the book concludes by guiding you through constructing your own birdhouses, feeders, and baths. You'll find step-by-step instructions and materials lists for DIY projects utilizing recycled items. Bringing the neighborhood together to build and install community bird sanctuaries is also covered. After reading this book, your appreciation for backyard birds will never be the same! Let's explore the wonders of birding in your own garden.

PART 1

HOW TO ATTRACT BIRDS TO YOUR GARDEN

| CHAPTER 1 |

THE ALLURE OF A BIRD-FRIENDLY GARDEN

Gardening is about more than just plants - it's about creating a space outdoors that nourishes the soul. For many gardeners, an important part of that is attracting beautiful birds to the yard. Watching colorful songbirds flit through the air, hearing their cheerful chirps and trills, seeing them splash in a birdbath or nibble seeds from a feeder - these simple pleasures connect us to nature and bring joy. Creating a bird-friendly garden has many emotional and mental health benefits.

The Emotional Benefits of Birding

Studies have shown that observing and interacting with birds can reduce stress, anxiety, and depression. The sights and sounds of wild birds seem to have a calming effect on the nervous system. Listening to birdsong first thing in the morning can be uplifting, starting your day off on a positive note. Watching the antics of feathered visitors at a backyard feeder provides lighthearted amusement. Spotting a flash of color as a cardinal darts past or hearing the twitter of chickadees fosters mindfulness, keeping you focused in the present moment. And identifying different bird species gives a sense of purpose and achievement. All of these small emotional boosts from birding add up, bolstering mental wellbeing.

In today's fast-paced, technology-driven world, finding opportunities to connect with nature is vital for maintaining balance and perspective. Birds are everywhere, even in cities, providing an easy way to tap into the natural rhythms of the earth. Tuning into the activity at a backyard bird feeder allows you to observe each season passing - the birds that come and go, their breeding colors and patterns, their feeding behaviors and migration habits. Caring for the birds that visit your garden forges a relationship with wild creatures, helping you feel part of the broader natural community. Watching over nesting birds feels akin to nurturing a family. And identifying fledglings each year gives a sense of continuity and renewal.

Why Birds Matter

In addition to the mental health benefits, attracting birds to your yard has ecological importance. As habitats for native birds dwindle, suburban and urban gardens can provide essential sanctuaries. Gardens landscaped with native plants that provide seeds, berries, nuts and nectar help sustain bird populations. Water sources like bird baths provide needed hydration. Thickets, brush piles, and evergreens offer shelter from predators and the elements. And nest boxes provide safe places to raise young. Your garden may represent only a small oasis, but the combined efforts of bird-friendly gardens across neighborhoods and towns can truly make a difference in conservation.

Beyond supporting birds, a bird-friendly garden also nurtures overall ecosystem health. Many birds play key roles in regulating insects, pollinating plants, and dispersing seeds. Robins, blue jays, and other species help control pest insects naturally, reducing the need for chemical pesticides. Hummingbirds, orioles, and grosbeaks transport pollen between flowers as they feed on nectar, aiding pollination. And birds consume berries and fruit, then spread the undigested seeds far and wide through their droppings. Providing habitat for birds inherently supports a balanced, sustainable garden ecology.

The Basics of Bird Behavior

To create an attractive environment for birds in your yard, it helps to understand some basics of their behavior. Different species have adapted to fill diverse ecological niches, developing optimal feeding, nesting, and social behaviors. Providing what each niche needs is key to birdscaping success.

Many songbirds in backyards are primarily seed eaters. Sparrows, finches, doves, juncos and more will avail themselves of seed from feeders as an easy food source. Woodpeckers thrive on suet, a high-energy food. Ground dwellers like towhees and juncos forage among leaf litter and dirt for dropped seeds.

Fruit, nectar and insects comprise key foods for other groups. Orioles seek out oranges, berries and sugary foods. Hummingbirds zip to flowers and feeders for nectar. Grosbeaks and waxwings devour fruit like dogwood and serviceberry. Flycatchers, warblers, and others snap up insects from foliage and branches. Various birds scavenge worms, grubs and larvae from soil. Providing foods to suit each dietary preference will satisfy diverse species.

In addition to eating behaviors, nesting preferences vary. Many songbirds like robins and chickadees nest in tree cavities or nest boxes. Cardinals, finches and phoebes build open twiggy nests in shrubs and trees. Ground-nesting birds like meadowlarks and killdeer lay eggs in shallow dirt scrapes. Adaptable song sparrows will nest just about anywhere. Offering suitable nesting sites provides birds with a secure place to raise their young. Provide cavities, dense vegetation, and open ground.

Birds also need cover for roosting and shelter. Evergreens, like pines, give winter protection and places to escape predators. Dense shrubs offer hiding spots from danger. Wood and brush piles provide retreats as well. Position cover strategically so birds always have a safe refuge.

Crafting a Bird Haven

With some thoughtful design, plant selections, and habitat features, you can convert your yard into a prime destination for many favorite feathered friends. Follow this advice for crafting a veritable bird paradise.

Food

To satisfy dietary needs, provide diverse food sources. Select plants offering seeds, like coneflowers, sunflowers, and prairie grasses. Grow berries on dogwoods, blueberries, viburnums and native shrubs. Plant nectar-rich flowers for hummingbirds and orioles like penstemons, monarda, salvia and trumpet vine. Add feeders with preferred seeds, suet cakes, nectar mixes, and fruit. Use native plants whenever possible.

Water

Install a birdbath, recirculating fountain, or garden pond. Make sure the water is just a few inches deep and kept clean. Place smooth stones inside for perching and add a mister for bathing. Site water sources in the open but near cover for safety.

Shelter

Allow native grasses and wildflowers to go to seed, leaving winter food and natural cover. Leave brush and wood piles for hiding spots. Plant evergreens like junipers and pines or dense hedges for windbreaks. Position bird houses and feeders near trees, shrubs or trellises so birds have escape cover.

Nesting

Install bird boxes tailored to specific species' needs. Face openings away from prevailing winds and intense sun but keep visible. Maintain boxes and clean them yearly. Allow dead trees to stand for nest cavities. Plant twiggy shrubs and small trees that birds can nest in. Avoid disturbing areas of dense ground vegetation so ground nesters aren't impacted.

Natural Pest Control

Minimize or eliminate pesticide use so ample insects thrive for natural bird food sources. Introduce native plants that support beneficial insect life cycles. Accept minor damage, knowing birds help keep pests in check. Provide habitat for birds like bats and swallows that eat flying insects.

Thank you for your purchase!

We extend our sincere gratitude for choosing "The Backyard Birding Bible"
as a part of your reading repertoire.

Scan this QR-CODE to get your **FREE BONUS BOOK** resource carefully curated
to deepen your understanding of essential homesteading practices,
self-sufficiency techniques, and strategies for cultivating a thriving homestead.

| CHAPTER 2 |

PLANTS AND TREES BIRDS LOVE

When designing a bird-friendly garden, choosing the right plants is key to enticing feathered visitors. Birds rely on vegetation for food sources, shelter from weather and predators, nesting sites, and perching spots. Selecting native plants tailored to your region and the needs of target bird species will transform your yard into an avian paradise.

Native Plants for Maximum Attraction

While ornamental imports may add visual interest, native plants have evolved side by side with local wildlife. They are adapted to thrive in your climate and soil, resisting disease and surviving weather extremes. Their flowers, fruits, nuts and seeds developed over eons to match regional bird and pollinator needs. And native insects like butterflies and moths rely completely on native flora for larval food. So, to create a healthy habitat for the widest diversity of birds, make native plants the foundation of your landscape.

When choosing natives, research options specific to your location that will support your favorite birds. Talk to staff at a local native plant nursery or natural history museum. Visit public parks and protected natural areas to see what grows well in wild spaces nearby. Observe yards in your neighborhood that already attract birds and make note of what's planted there. Then select native trees, shrubs, vines, grasses and flowering plants that provide what birds in your area seek:

Seed and Berries

Many perching songbirds dine on small seeds and berries. Fruit from dogwood, hollies, sumac and viburnum sustain birds through winter. Herbaceous native plants like asters, sunflowers, coneflowers and goldenrods produce abundant seeds. Even allowing native grasses and sedges to go to seed provides essential winter provisions.

Nectar

To draw nectar lovers like hummingbirds and orioles, choose native plants with tubular red, orange or yellow blooms. Trumpet creeper, penstemon, monarda, and columbine are prime examples, along with certain sages, honeysuckles and wild buckwheats. Have blooms over a long season by planting early and late-blooming varieties.

Foliage and Twigs

Native trees and shrubs offer leaves and twigs as food sources. Elms, birches, maples and oaks support caterpillars that many birds relish. Fruit trees provide buds in early spring. Allow some dead twigs and branches to remain for birds to browse.

Shelter

Evergreens, dense shrubs, tall grasses and vine-covered trellises provide shelter from harsh weather and concealment from predators. Birds also seek refuge by nesting in thickets and hollows.

Cavities

Woodpeckers create nest holes in dead trees that secondary hole nesters later use. Allow snags to stand and avoid removing dead branches on live trees. Native plants have naturally occurring cavities and crevices that birds utilize.

Trees as Natural Bird Feeders

Including some tree varieties favored by birds will exponentially increase activity as they dine on buds, fruit and the insects trees attract. Consider adding these arboreal all-stars:

Crabapples

These small ornamental apples bear arching branches laden with bright red fruit beloved by robins, waxwings, cardinals, blue jays and more. Grow a few different cultivars for an extended harvest. Plant near cover for a quick escape from predators. Crabapples also have showy spring blossoms.

Oaks

Acorns are a high-calorie food source for chickadees, woodpeckers, flickers and game birds like turkey and grouse. Oaks host plentiful insects to feed flycatchers, warblers and others. Their loose, open branching frames make good perches and song posts. White and swamp oaks work well in wet soils.

Maples

Warblers and vireos glean insects from the dense, twiggy branching of maples. Hummingbirds tap early flowing sap. Maples have winged fruit that whirligigs, sparrows and cardinals all enjoy. The shading canopy also helps keep your yard cool.

Serviceberries

Also called Juneberries, serviceberries are practically bird magnets. Their white spring blossoms provide nectar. Warblers and vireos use branch fork nest sites. The summer fruit feast attracts robins, waxwings, thrashers and more. Foliage turns a fiery orange and red in fall.

Dogwoods

Berries of flowering dogwoods ripen late when other food sources are scarce, sustaining migrants and overwintering birds. Showy spring blooms support pollinators. Dogwoods provide good nesting sites, too. Plants where the tiered horizontal branching can spread naturally.

Hackberries

These hardy, disease-resistant trees have an open form that invites birds. The tiny fig-like fruit draws in flocks of robins, waxwings, woodpeckers and more to the banquet. Hackberries adapt well to a wide range of soils and climates.

Mulberries

Catbirds, brown thrashers, orioles and dozens more will flock to the hanging clusters of juicy berries on mulberry trees. They grow with abandon, providing ample fruit and spreading shade. Birds devour them right off the branch and off the ground. Mulberries thrive with neglect in nearly any soil.

Hollies

Evergreen hollies offer shelter all year round, as well as abundant red berries that persist into winter. They become a vital food source for mockingbirds, robins, bluebirds and others when the ground is frozen or snow-covered. Plant varieties with ample fruit like winterberry and possumhaw.

Birches

Chickadees, grosbeaks and many woodland birds seek out birch trees. They eat the seeds and bud scales in spring, foraging insects from the foliage and gleaning seeds from conelike fruit in fall and winter. Paper and river birches boast striking white trunks.

Flowering Plants Birds Adore

In addition to trees, include plenty of flowering native plants to provide nectar, pollen, seeds and the insects drawn to blooms. Aim for a succession of flowers from early spring through late fall to sustain migrating and year-round birds. Here are some top picks:

Columbine

Hummingbirds cruise the long, nectar-filled blooms of columbine as they migrate north in spring. Orioles and native bees visit, too. And songbirds, like finches, eat the seeds as they mature. Columbine self-sows freely in light shade.

Beebalm

With shaggy masses of tubular flowers in shades of red, pink, orange and purple, beebalm is an absolute must for a bird-friendly garden. Hummingbirds, orioles, butterflies and bees feast on the nectar throughout summer.

Penstemon

Also called beardtongue, penstemon flowers have just the right shape for hummingbird beaks to access their abundant nectar. Tubular blooms come in reds, purples, pinks and whites. Penstemon thrives in full sun and tolerates drought well once established.

Cardinal flower

Named for its bright red tubular flowers loved by hummingbirds and northern cardinals, this moisture-loving native thrives along ponds, streams and rain gardens. The vertical spikes of cardinal flowers bloom from midsummer into fall.

Blazing stars

Clouds of small purple flowers cover the blazing star's upright stalks for months, attracting hummingbirds and butterflies galore. Finches and sparrows eat the seeds once flowers fade. Blazing stars are easy to grow, tolerating any soil and thriving in prairie landscapes.

Blue sage

Azure blue flowers of aromatic blue sage are a late summer buffet for hummingbirds before migration. Orioles also stop by to partake. The shrublike clumping form works well in borders. Full sun and good drainage keep it blooming happily.

Goldenrods

Don't weed out goldenrods - their bright golden sprays of blossom nourish migrating hummingbirds in late summer and early fall. Seeds provide food for finches and others all winter long. These easy-care plants thrive in poor soils and bloom for weeks.

Asters

Dainty flowers of asters in hues of violet, fuchsia, magenta and white light up fall gardens. Their nectar sustains migrating hummers and resident orioles. Seeds feed chickadees, juncos and sparrows once they fade. New England, aromatic and calico asters are some top species.

Sunflowers

Giant sunflower blooms provide nectar for orioles, finches and woodpeckers. Chickadees, cardinals and jays feast on the hearty seeds within. Plant some towering cultivars as well as native Maximillian and Jerusalem artichokes for late blooms.

CHAPTER 3

WATER FEATURES AND THEIR ATTRACTION

The sight and sound of running water irresistibly draws birds in. Adding a water feature to your garden exponentially increases its appeal, enticing both feathered and human visitors alike. Water sources provide birds with a place to bathe, drink, splash and cool off. The presence of water also attracts insects, amphibians, and other creatures birds prey on, so activity increases dramatically around well-sited pools and fountains. With some thoughtful planning, you can incorporate water features tailored to your space, budget and desires that will truly make your garden sing with avian life.

Ponds, Streams, and Waterfalls

While any water source has appeal, ponds, streams and waterfalls take it up a notch. The sound of trickling or splashing water is like a siren song to birds, calling them from afar. Ponds and streams also allow more birds to drink and bathe at once. And moving water helps prevent stagnation and mosquito problems. Here are some top tips for adding ponds and watercourses to your garden:

Ponds

An in-ground or above-ground pond with varying depths allows birds to choose bathing depths but includes shallow zones for drinking and safety. Ramp slopes provide easy access. Include a mix of open water and aquatic plants like water lilies for beauty and habitat. Strategically place large stones for perching and as escape routes. Site ponds in light shade near bushes, trees or shrubs.

Streams

Mimic nature by contouring and lining a streambed to meander through your garden. Pea gravel, small boulders and pond liner create the watercourse. Add recirculating pumps in sequenced pools, moving water over rocky obstructions to generate pleasing sounds. Ensure a shallow flow over most of the length for bird safety and plants like rushes or irises.

Waterfalls

Siting a small preformed waterfall at one end of a pond adds visual and auditory dynamism. Or you can construct a faux stream bank and line it with rocks to create a naturalistic waterfall. Using pumps, make water cascade over the stones into a splash zone below. The white noise blocks modern sounds and creates a sanctuary vibe.

Garden feng shui principles recommend placing water in the front of your home or garden, pointing toward the house. But most importantly, site water where it's visible from indoors and your favorite outdoor spaces so you can enjoy the show. Position water features near cover like trees, tall grasses or large boulders for bird safety, too. Then kick back and watch your mini oasis come to life!

Regular Maintenance Tips

To keep backyard water elements clean and safe for birds over the long term, some periodic maintenance is required. Follow these tips:

- Change water frequently, or use filters and aquatic plants to maintain freshness naturally
- Remove fallen leaves, dead vegetation, and bird/animal waste promptly
- Keep pumps and filtration systems running properly

- Clean out sediment buildup from the pond bottom
- Prune back overgrown plants to keep areas open
- Treat algae if it becomes excessive with commercial products
- Wash birdbaths and fountains weekly with soap and water, rinsing thoroughly
- Empty and fully air-dry baths/fountains weekly to control bacterial growth
- Brush and scrub mineral buildup and grime from rocks and statues
- In winter, use a de-icer designed for birdbaths to keep ice-free
- Repair any cracks or leaks promptly to maintain water levels

While a bit of green algae growth provides a natural look, too much buildup of organic matter, waste and algae creates an unhealthy environment. So invest some time regularly in cleaning and maintenance. The benefits for your garden's appeal and ecosystem will repay your efforts manifold.

Add the Magic of Water

Incorporating ponds, streams, waterfalls or simple birdbaths into your landscape provides vital sustenance for birds and brings tranquil beauty into your garden. The sight of splashing birds at your unique water feature will soon have you hooked! With some mindful planning and care, you can create a refreshing oasis for wildlife that nourishes the soul as it invites feathered friends to stay awhile. The magic and joy water features evoke are well worth the effort. Your garden will overflow with life, serenity and song when you add the allure of water.

CHAPTER 4

BIRDS' FAVORITE FOODS AND HOW TO PROVIDE THEM

A key way to draw diverse birds to visit and linger in your garden is by offering enticing foods they crave. Different bird species have adapted beaks and feeding behaviors perfectly suited to specific diets. Catering to those preferences will satisfy birds and help them thrive. This chapter will cover the main diet categories to appeal to various birds, explain what to feed seasonally, and provide tips on using natural food sources and protecting birds at feeders. Follow this advice for a foolproof feeding strategy.

Types of Bird Feed

Seeds: Many common feeder birds like sparrows, finches, doves and juncos primarily eat small seeds. These birds have short, chunky beaks adept at cracking open seeds and husking them. Different species prefer certain seeds like nyger thistle, millet, safflower, sunflower kernels, cracked corn, milo and more. Watch what gets eaten fastest in your yard and adjust offerings accordingly. Use high-quality seed blends and include some variety to attract more species. Platform feeders, hopper feeders and tube feeders with short perches suit seed lovers best. Scatter some seeds on the ground for juncos and doves.

Suet

Woodpeckers, nuthatches, chickadees, wrens and others thrive on suet, which is the fat and marrow from animal sources. Suet provides quick energy in cold weather. Offer suet cakes, plugs or loose suet in cage feeders tailored to clingers. Look for no-melt suet in warm months. Situate suet feeding stations near trees so birds can perch before and after eating.

Fruit

Robins, waxwings, bluebirds, orioles, tanagers and other colorful fruit lovers visit gardens when berries and fruits abound. Include native fruiting trees and shrubs in landscape plans. Also, offer sliced oranges, apples and bananas in platform feeders with fruit cage attachments. Avoid dried fruit, which can dehydrate birds.

Nectar

To attract hummingbirds and orioles, fill specialty nectar feeders with sugar/water mixes formulated for these birds. Use red feeders to draw hummers and orange for orioles. Clean nectar feeders weekly to prevent spoilage. Supplement feeders with plenty of flowering native plants, changing up blooms to provide spring through fall food.

Insects

Chickadees, wrens, thrushes, warblers and flycatchers pursue insects from trees and shrubs. Allow deadwood to stand and avoid pesticides so insect populations can thrive. Plant native flowering trees and shrubs that attract the most insects. Also, include an insect feeding station stocked with live mealworms to supplement natural prey.

No-waste foods like nectar and suet offer efficiency for birds and ease for you. But also provide seeds so birds get balanced nutrition. Consider each species' unique needs and cater to those preferences. Offering a variety of feeder types and foods will satisfy the tastes of diverse feathered visitors.

Seasonal Feeding Recommendations

As seasons change, so do the energy needs of wild birds. Follow this advice on switching up food offerings throughout the year:

Spring

In spring, migrating birds rely heavily on insects and nectar from flowering plants after their long journeys. Offering sugar water mixes in nectar feeders provides carbohydrates for fuel. Make sure flowering trees, shrubs and plants are available too. Birds raising young also need more protein, so include suet cakes and mealworms.

Summer

Keep nectar feeders freshly stocked for nesting hummers and orioles. Offer fruits like oranges and berries. Seeds and suet remain important for young birds and molting adults. Also, ensure plenty of natural insects by avoiding pesticides and letting dead plants stand. Install a water mister for bathing opportunities.

Fall

In autumn, migrating birds need ample food reserves for travel, so higher-calorie suet, nuts and seeds are important. Keep feeders full as birds pass through your area. Fruit trees and shrubs laden with ripe berries provide portable nutrition. Fatten birds up before seasonal declines.

Winter

Food can be scarce in winter, making full feeders a lifeline during freezing weather. Prioritize high-fat foods like suet, peanuts and nyger thistle seed. Offer ample black oil sunflower for cardinals and jays. Put out extra no-waste seed cakes and cylinders so birds can find them when snow covers the ground. Also, clear ice buildup from birdbaths regularly with a deicer.

The Role of Natural Prey

While bird feeders provide useful supplemental nutrition, birds rely heavily on natural insect prey to feed themselves and their young. Supporting healthy native insect populations in your yard is crucial.

Limit pesticide usage, even natural versions, so insect numbers and diversity can thrive. Remove invasive plant species that disrupt ecosystems. Allow some dead plant matter like fallen leaves and dried stalks to decompose in place instead of overcleaning a garden. And plant native species that coevolved with local insect varieties.

Shrubs like native hawthorns, blackberries and wild roses attract abundant insects. Trees like oak, maple and willow host caterpillars birds prize. Milkweed and other wildflowers nourish butterfly and moth larvae. A fallen dead tree chock full of burrows and holes offers nesting spots for insects. A pile of downed branches provides habitat. A patch of leaf litter holds beetles, ants and spiders. Diverse native plants support diverse insect life that forms the base of the food web.

Also include special bird feeding stations just for insects. You can buy live mealworms, grubs and other insects at pet and nature stores. Serve them up in special feeders. Also, make your own "bug butter" to smear on branches or logs by mixing together peanuts, lard, flour, sugar and freeze-dried insects. The birds will thank you for setting out these insect "appetizers" along with their seed or suet entrees.

Avoiding Predators at Feeders

Feeders draw in not only welcome birds but also clever predators like hawks, cats, raccoons and snakes. Use these strategies to protect birds:

Site feeders in open spots away from dense cover where ambush predators hide and wait. Prune lower branches on nearby shrubs and trees to eliminate lurking spots. Clear debris from the ground beneath feeders regularly.

Install feeders near windows so you can monitor activity and scare off unwanted guests. Position feeders closer to your house and well-lit doorways or patios rather than borders near woods and brush.

Choose feeder styles made of steel wire that prevents access for larger animals. Use metal guards over feeding ports and hang feeders on long pipes that deter animals from climbing. Avoid feeders mounted on the ground.

Plant shrubs and trees densely on the perimeter of your lot to deter stalking from woods or brush, but keep feeder zones open. Set up plastic owls or flashing pie pans in trees to startle predators away.

Remove cat and dog food from outdoors after pets eat so it doesn't draw wildlife near the house. Keep pet doors closed and supervise cats outdoors to protect birds. Use cat-repellent plants like rosemary and lavender around feeders.

Check feeders at dusk and dawn when predators are active. Scare them off with loud noises, or chase them out of your yard. Take feeders in at night to avoid nocturnal poachers.

Selectively prune trees and shrubs to open up sight lines and eliminate protective cover near feeders. Trim back overhanging branches above feeders to prevent ambush from above. Avoid using fencing, netting or wire that birds could collide with.

PART 2

RECORDING BIRDS IN YOUR GARDEN

| CHAPTER 1 |
SETTING UP A
BIRD JOURNAL

Birdwatching is an immensely rewarding hobby, allowing enthusiasts to connect with nature, observe fascinating bird behaviors, and contribute to conservation efforts. One of the fundamental tools for birdwatchers is a bird journal. In this chapter, we will explore the reasons for keeping a bird journal, the choice between analog and digital mediums, the value of sketching as an observation tool, and various templates and layouts to help beginners get started.

Why Journal?

Keeping a bird journal can be an extremely rewarding activity for any bird enthusiast or backyard bird watcher. There are many benefits to journaling your bird observations, encounters and activities. Here are some of the top reasons to start a bird journal:

Improves Observation Skills

One of the best reasons to keep a bird journal is that it trains you to become a more careful, detail-oriented observer. Good bird watching requires close attention and observation skills. As you regularly journal, you will find that you become better at noticing small physical details, behaviors, sounds and other characteristics of the birds around you. Your journal keeps you engaged and present in each bird encounter. Over time, you can look back on your records and see how much your observation skills have improved!

Tracks Change Over Time

A journal creates a long-term record that allows you to track patterns and changes over weeks, months or years. Look back on your entries to see how your backyard bird populations change throughout the seasons. Notice migration patterns, nesting behaviors, feeding activities and more. See how your garden ecology transforms each year and how it impacts the birds that visit. Without a journal, it's impossible to recall all these details.

Creates a Personalized Record

Your journal documents your unique local bird life. While field guides and bird books describe species in general terms, your journal chronicles the specific bird individuals and behaviors that you encounter in your unique environment. The dates, details and specifics in your journal create a personalized record of the birds, your property, seasonal changes and bird activity unique to your context.

Provides Accountability

Keeping a journal creates accountability to get outside regularly and make careful observations. When you make bird watching and journaling a consistent habit, you will notice much more compared to casual, occasional or scattered observations. You'll be motivated to watch carefully, record new findings, and continue expanding your journal entries on a regular basis.

Memory Aid

Our memories are imperfect. A journal helps you accurately recall details that would otherwise be forgotten. Re-read your notes to remind yourself of sightings, facts and numbers that may have faded from memory. Refer back to refresh your memory on species identification, appearance, behaviors, visits and patterns.

Tracks Your Progress

Look back on your older journal entries to see how much you've learned over time. As your knowledge, skills and experience grow, your journaling will reflect your increasing abilities to identify birds, understand behavior, and notice subtle details. Appreciate how far you've come!

Fosters Appreciation and Curiosity

Focusing intently on recording bird observations makes you appreciate the wonder of birdlife and fuels your curiosity to keep learning. Keeping a journal inspires you to slow down, watch patiently, find joy in bird behaviors and discover something new. Referring back to your records reminds you of special encounters and memorable moments.

Creates a Record for Future Generations

While personal now, your journals could one day serve as valuable data for local environmental history. Recording your regular observations over the years documents bird life over time in your corner of the world. These firsthand observations could inform future scientists, conservationists, community members or descendants interested in changes in backyard birds over the decades.

Analog vs. Digital: Choosing Your Medium

When deciding how to record your bird observations and journals, you have two main options - analog or digital. Both have their own sets of pros and cons. Here are some things to consider when choosing which method is right for you:

Analog Journal

The classic way to keep naturalist field notes is with an old-fashioned paper journal. Use any notebook or bound journal that appeals to you. Some birders enjoy the vintage aesthetic of a leather field notebook. Others prefer a simple student composition book or spiral notebook. Select lined, graph or blank pages - whichever you find most suitable. This allows you to record handwritten log entries on paper with drawings, tape in items like feathers or pressed flowers, and more.

Digital Journal

Alternatively, you can keep a digital birding journal on a smartphone, tablet, laptop or desktop computer. Use a general word processing program, spreadsheet, birding app, or online platform. This allows you to type up notes for each entry. You can also insert photos, audio clips, and other media seamlessly. Digital files are easily searchable, backed up, and take up no physical space.

Sketching as a Tool for Observation

Recording written details is central to a good bird journal, but don't underestimate the value of sketches, too. Adding simple illustrations of your bird encounters and observations can enhance your journal in many ways. Here are some of the benefits of sketching birds and their behaviors:

Improves Observation Skills

Just like writing details in a journal, carefully sketching a bird focuses on your awareness and observation abilities. As you sketch field marks, shapes, proportions and other visual qualities, you train your eye and perceptive skills. You'll find yourself noticing subtleties that you miss by observation alone. Drawing demands close attention to details like feather patterns, bill shapes, subtle colors, movements and more.

Engages Different Parts of the Brain

Writing is primarily a left-brain activity. But sketching engages more right-brain creativity and spatial processing. Drawing birds engages brain activity and develops visual-spatial skills in ways that just writing does not. The combination of left-brain written observation notes plus right-brain drawing creates a more complete record and a great learning experience.

Provides Visual Details Hard to Describe in Words

While descriptions are essential in a bird journal, some details are hard to capture accurately in words alone. Quick sketches illustrate plumage markings, bill shapes, behaviors, relative size, greenery, weather elements, spatial relationships and other visual qualities that words may fail to convey. A simple drawing can communicate volumes.

Makes Journal More Personal

Unlike field guide drawings, your sketches reflect your personal eye, drawing style and real-time field impressions. They add a unique personal touch and intimacy to your journal. Your drawings will get better over time, too! Looking back on older sketches shows your artistic progress.

Slows You Down

Sketching is a slow, methodical process compared to quick written notes. Taking the time to sketch intuitively makes you slow down, observe patiently, and absorb more details. This attentiveness leads to a richer understanding of bird appearance and behavior.

Captures Action and Behavior

Sketches can illustrate bird postures, movements, interactions, flight dynamics, feeding behaviors and much more that words may not adequately describe. Quick sketches of birds in action provide a unique glimpse into avian activity.

Allows Creativity

Drawing allows you to be creative in how you summarize and share your observations. While aiming for accuracy, you can also have fun and experiment with different illustration styles. Quick gesture drawings, detailed studies, whimsical cartoons, simple diagrams, abstract designs - enjoy the creative process!

Tells a Story

A journal entry with sketches helps convey a narrative and brings the encounter to life on the page. Drawings complement your written observations to tell a richer, more vivid story of each bird-watching excursion.

Provides Artistic Joy

For many nature lovers, combining art with science brings great joy and satisfaction. The act of sketching birds, plants and habitats provides a wonderful creative outlet. In a world of digital tech, making art by hand is rejuvenating.

Templates and Layouts for Starters

If facing a blank page feels daunting, using a template can help provide helpful guidance on setting up your birding journal pages. Here are some easy layouts and systems to give you a good start:

Header Template

Start each page or journal entry with a header block that captures key metadata:

Date: [Full date]

Time: [Start and end time of observation]

Location: [Be specific with the name of the park, your backyard, street name, city, GPS coordinates, etc.]

Habitat: [Brief notes about vegetation, urban/natural, weather, water sources, etc.]

This header gives vital context about when and where the sighting took place. Make it a habit to fill this in first before your main entry.

Log Template

For clean, organized daily logs, use a table or grid format:

[Header]

Time - Species - Qty - Details

7:05 am - American Robin - 2 - Adult pair foraging on the lawn

7:23 am - Black-capped Chickadee - 1 - Calling and perched on the feeder

8:30 am - Downy Woodpecker - 1 - Male drilling on suet cage

etc.

This log style works well for quick, efficient daily records. Leave blank rows to add species times later.

Expanded Template

For a more in-depth entry on a featured observation, try:

[Header]

Field Marks:

[Include physical description, key features, the size relative to known species, etc.]

Behavior:
[Make detailed notes on what the bird is doing, interactions, movements, flight style, etc.]

Sounds:
[Describe songs, chip notes, wing sounds, etc. Include mnemonics that help you recall sound patterns.]

Sketch:
[Simple sketch of the profile, unique marks, behavior, habitat, etc.]

This expanded template pushes you to slow down and record more complete notes for special sightings.

CHAPTER 2
TOOLS AND APPS FOR BIRD RECORDING

In the ever-evolving world of birdwatching, the advent of modern technology has significantly enhanced the experience for enthusiasts. Gone are the days when birding solely relied on the keen eyes and ears of naturalists. Today, tools and apps have revolutionized the way we record and document bird species in our gardens. In this chapter, we will explore the exciting intersection of technology and bird recording, delving into modern tech for old-fashioned birding, popular apps for recording, equipment for sound recording, and software for analysis. By the end of this comprehensive guide, you will be well-equipped to embark on your bird recording journey with confidence and precision.

Modern Tech for Old-Fashioned Birding

While traditional pencil and paper can never be replaced, modern technology opens up exciting new possibilities for recording and analyzing bird observations. A wide array of digital tools now assist both novice birders and scientists alike in documenting avian species.

Apps, audio recorders, advanced optics, mapping software, databases, and more all leverage the capabilities of technology to enhance bird watching and research. When used appropriately, these digital aids deepen knowledge and engagement with birds versus detracting from direct experience.

Approach new tech with an open mind. Be selective in adding tools that genuinely assist your goals rather than just accumulating gadgets. Thoughtfully incorporate the most useful tech to amplify the rewarding feelings of connecting with nature.

Binoculars and Spotting Scopes

Quality optics like binoculars and spotting scopes are excellent technical aids for observation. Binoculars offer portability and wide fields of view. Spotting scopes provide more powerful magnification for distant subjects.

Consider model specifications like magnification power, objective lens size, field of view, eye relief, weight, waterproofing and more to choose the best instrument for your needs and budget. Test different models in person when possible. Invest in the best optics you can afford from reputable brands.

Use optics judiciously, and don't over-rely on them. Put down your binoculars to engage birds with your natural senses as well. Think of them as tools to provide clarity and detail when needed while still immersing yourself in the overall experience.

Cameras and Telephoto Lenses

Digital cameras with telephoto lenses allow you to capture diagnostic photos to aid in identification or to supplement your written and sketched observations. They also provide you with beautiful avian images to inspire and share with others.

Choose a camera with quick autofocus, burst modes, and good low-light capabilities to photograph active, fast-moving birds. DSLR cameras offer interchangeable lenses for maximum versatility. Smaller mirrorless or point-and-shoot cameras provide greater portability.

Photograph responsibly so your presence doesn't disrupt bird behavior. Do your research to pick camera features optimized for wildlife and bird photography.

Audio Recording Gear

Quality audio recordings of bird vocalizations are an invaluable supplement to written and visual observations. Small handheld recorders from brands like Sony and Zoom offer affordability, simplicity and great results.

For more advanced recording, consider a shotgun microphone that can be mounted on a camera and focused directly at a vocalizing bird. Wind screens reduce noise and interference. Portable field mixers allow you to control multiple mics and audio sources.

Having the ability to capture clear audio clips to refer back to later aids immensely in learning bird songs, calls, flight sounds and other auditory birding cues.

Mapping Tools

Applications like Google Maps allow you to precisely record locations where you observe birds by dropping pins at exact coordinates of sightings. This helps you identify patterns and high-activity areas.

Other tools like eBird track your sightings on interactive maps, allowing you to visualize where you have birded and contribute data points to science. Apps access GPS data to auto-pinpoint bird locations as well.

Range and Habitat Maps

Referencing range maps shows you the geographic breeding and living areas for each bird species. This allows you to better understand the regional behaviors and movements you observe.

Consult habitat preference maps to determine what types of food, water, cover, elevation, climate and other resources various species tend to favor. Compare these to your location.

Digital Field Guides

A number of digital field guides offer advantages over traditional book guides. Search tools help you quickly filter long species lists by location, color, size and other attributes to narrow ID. The quiz and game features test identification skills. Embedded videos and audio provide helpful visual and auditory learning aides right in the app.

Consider still keeping a physical guide with you to reference in the field when phone batteries die. But multi-media-rich apps are great complements for learning.

Popular Apps for Recording

Specialized apps offer user-friendly, portable ways to log in and learn about birds in the field. Here are some top-rated iOS and Android apps for tech-assisted birding:

eBird

The world's most popular birding app, eBird, provides tools to record bird sightings and explore vast crowdsourced data. Log checklists from anywhere and maintain thorough life lists. Data contributes to science and conservation. Includes regional bird abundance graphics, hotspot maps, and rarity alerts.

Merlin Bird ID

Merlin asks a series of simple questions to provide spot-on bird identification assistance. Along with ID, it offers photos, sounds, range maps and other learning content. Captivating quizzes improve skills. Great for beginners and experts alike. Developed by the Cornell Lab of Ornithology.

iNaturalist

Contribute observations across nature to this community science app and help scientists track biodiversity. AI assists with species ID, and data is verified by the community. Connect with other naturalists and nature lovers to learn and discuss.

Audubon Bird Guide

Comprehensive profiles, photos, audio, video and ID tips for over 800 North American species. Create life lists and log sightings. Filters, quizzes, monthly bird forecasts and more. Developed by the National Audubon Society.

Sibley Birds

The entire catalog of illustrations and content from the famous Sibley field guide was brought to life digitally. Compare similar species visually with 4000+ artworks. Focuses solely on North American birds.

Bird Song ID USA

Includes a collection of 600 bird song recordings with spectrogram visuals and species details to master auditory ID skills. Listen to vocalizations and test yourself with review quizzes.

Seek by iNaturalist

Snap a photo of any organism (bird or other) while out exploring, and the app's image recognition will suggest an identification in seconds. Great for casual nature watchers and kids.

BirdNET

Identify birds by recording their sounds. The app listens and analyzes vocalizations to provide likely ID matches. Also, documents and tracks recordings.

Peterson Birds

The digital version of a popular field guide covers species with range maps, audio, photos and videos. Filter by shape, color and location to simplify identification.

Bird Buddy

Smart AI-powered camera and app that recognizes and identifies birds visiting your backyard in real-time. Gets to know regular visitors. Beginner-friendly.

Some apps like eBird and Merlin focus on functionality for logging and identifying sightings. Others like Sibley and Peterson provide comprehensive visual field guides. Several emphasize learning birds by song. Try different apps to see which user experience and features best match your needs and style.

The best birding apps leverage technology thoughtfully to open new possibilities for discovering and learning avian natural history. Let them supplement - but not replace - your innate curiosity and direct connection to the natural world.

Equipment for Sound Recording

Listening carefully and identifying birds by ear is an essential birding skill. Beyond annotations in your journal, recording audio clips of vocalizations provides helpful documentation to review later and improve auditory ID abilities over time.

You don't need fancy equipment to get started. Here are some easy tools for recording bird sounds:

Handheld Recorders

Affordable handheld recording devices from Sony, Zoom and Tascam provide crisp, clear audio well-suited for field recording nature sounds. Models under $100 offer surprisingly good quality.

Shotgun Microphones

Attaching a directional shotgun microphone to your camera allows you to isolate and focus on bird vocalizations and reduce ambient noise. Models from Audio-Technica, Rode and Sennheiser offer excellent quality without breaking the bank.

Parabolic Microphones

Parabolic reflector microphones further amplify and isolate sounds from a specific direction. Positioned properly, they enable recording birds from very far distances. Useful for timid or endangered species.

Portable Field Mixers

For advanced users, field mixers like the Sound Devices MixPre series provide inputs for multiple microphones and fine control over audio capture in the field. They take bird recording to the next level.

Windscreens and Pop Filters

Add windscreens, fuzzy covers, and pop filters on microphones to reduce noise from wind and plosives while enhancing vocal recordings. Critical for outdoor field recording.

Headphones

Listen to recordings through over-ear headphones to detect subtle details and differences. Earbuds lack the full sound range for critical audio analysis.

Poles and Mounts

Microphones attached on elevated poles and flexible mounts positioned nearer to vocalizing birds significantly improve recording quality from distant subjects in the field.

Ultra-directional Microphones

Cutting-edge parabolic dish microphones from companies like Telinga and Mikrofon enable extremely narrow focus for isolating and recording distant bird sounds with incredible clarity.

As with optics, carefully choose only the ideal equipment for your recording needs. Thoughtfully used alongside traditional birding skills, audio recorders allow us to tune in more intimately to birdsong and the acoustic environment.

Using Software for Analysis

Recording bird sounds is a fascinating and rewarding endeavor, but its true potential is unlocked through careful analysis of the captured audio. Analyzing bird sounds allows birdwatchers and ornithologists to delve deeper into the behaviors, communication patterns, and ecological roles of different bird species. Modern advancements in technology have significantly enhanced the analysis process, providing a plethora of software tools tailored to this purpose.

Key Software Applications for Bird Sound Analysis

Raven Pro

Developed by the Cornell Lab of Ornithology, Raven Pro is a widely used software for analyzing animal sounds, including bird vocalizations. It offers a range of tools for visualization, measurement, and annotation of sound recordings. Raven Pro is ideal for researchers and ornithologists conducting in-depth bioacoustic studies.

Audacity

Audacity is a free, open-source audio editing software that serves as a versatile tool for analyzing bird sound recordings. It allows users to visualize and edit audio files, apply filters, measure parameters, and even perform frequency analysis. Audacity is user-friendly and is a popular choice among both amateur and professional bird sound enthusiasts.

Adobe Audition

Adobe Audition is a professional-grade audio editing software that offers advanced tools for in-depth analysis of bird sound recordings. Ornithologists can utilize their precise control over audio parameters, noise reduction features, and spectral analysis tools to extract valuable information from recordings. Despite being a subscription-based service, its extensive capabilities make it a preferred choice for researchers requiring sophisticated audio editing.

Sonic Visualizer

Sonic Visualizer is a free, open-source software designed for the analysis of audio recordings, including bird sounds. It enables users to view and analyze the spectrogram of audio files, facilitating the identification of patterns and characteristics of different bird vocalizations. Its user-friendly interface and broad range of functionalities make it a valuable tool for bird sound analysis.

Xeno-Canto

While not traditional analysis software, Xeno-Canto is an online community-driven platform that allows bird sound enthusiasts to upload, share, and listen to bird recordings. Ornithologists often use this platform for comparing and identifying bird sounds, contributing to a global repository of bird vocalizations.

The Analysis Process

The process of analyzing bird sounds involves several steps to extract meaningful insights:

Recording and Collection

Bird sounds are recorded using specialized audio recording equipment, such as digital audio recorders and microphones. These recordings are then organized and stored for further analysis.

Importing into Software

The recorded audio files are imported into the chosen analysis software, where they can be visualized and manipulated for analysis.

Visualization

The software generates visual representations of the audio, such as spectrograms, waveforms, and pitch curves. These visualizations aid in understanding the frequency, intensity, and patterns of bird vocalizations.

Analysis and Interpretation

Ornithologists analyze the visual representations, measuring parameters such as pitch, frequency, call duration, and intervals between calls. They identify unique patterns, behaviors, and species based on the analysis.

Documentation and Reporting

The findings from the analysis are documented, and reports are generated to summarize the results. These reports often include spectrogram images, audio clips, and interpretations, providing a comprehensive overview of the analyzed bird sounds.

CHAPTER 3

TIPS FOR DAILY OBSERVATIONS

Birdwatching is an exhilarating hobby that connects individuals with the vibrant natural world. Observing and recording birds in your garden can provide deep insights into the behavior and patterns of these creatures. This chapter covers the best times for bird watching, bird behavior throughout the day, recording weather patterns, and the significance of long-term observations with a focus on seasonal changes.

Best Times for Bird Watching

Birdwatching is a pursuit deeply rooted in the natural rhythms of the environment. To truly appreciate the avian wonders in your garden, understanding the best times for bird watching is essential. These optimal periods provide a window into the avian world, where one can witness a kaleidoscope of behaviors and interactions that define the lives of birds.

Early Mornings: A Symphony of Awakening

The early morning, often referred to as the 'golden hour,' is a time when the world is just beginning to stir. The skies gradually lighten, and the first rays of the sun pierce through the darkness. This period is magical for birdwatchers, marking the beginning of a new day in the avian realm.

The dawn chorus is a hallmark of early mornings. Birds engage in a harmonious cacophony of songs and calls, creating a symphony that resonates through the air. Each species contributes its unique melody, creating a beautiful ensemble of sound. This symphony serves multiple purposes for the birds, including territorial marking, communication, and courtship displays.

As the day breaks, birds are enthusiastic and energized, eager to commence their daily activities. Foraging and feeding are their primary goals during these early hours. They flit from tree to tree, scouring for insects, seeds, and other sources of nourishment. Observing this frenetic activity provides insights into their dietary preferences, hunting techniques, and competition for food.

Late Afternoons: Preparing for Rest

Late afternoons are another prime time for birdwatching, often considered the 'golden hour' of the evening. The sun begins its descent, casting long shadows and painting the sky with hues of red and orange. The air cools, and the atmosphere becomes tranquil.

During this time, birds are engaged in last-minute preparations for the approaching night. Having expended their energy throughout the day, they now focus on foraging to replenish their reserves for the overnight period. Observing their feeding frenzies and interactions provides valuable insights into their feeding habits and social dynamics.

Birds engaging in their pre-sleep rituals are a common sight during late afternoons. They preen their feathers meticulously, ensuring their plumage is in optimum condition. This not only aids in flight but also serves as a means of maintaining insulation and staying warm during the night. Additionally, bathing activities are prevalent during this time, aiding in hygiene and feather maintenance.

Midday: A Moment of Calm

Midday, particularly around noon, represents a lull in bird activity. The sun is at its peak, and the temperature is often at its highest. Birds tend to seek shade and rest during this period to conserve energy and avoid the scorching heat.

During this quiet interlude, birdwatchers can still observe birds, albeit with a calmer demeanor. Many birds find shelter in the foliage, perching in the shade to escape the intensity of the sun. They engage in preening and grooming, keeping their feathers in top condition. Socializing and brief interactions may still occur, but the pace is significantly slower compared to the morning and late afternoon.

Some bird species, particularly those adapted to hot climates, may be more active during midday. Raptors, for instance, often take advantage of the thermals that form during this time to glide effortlessly in the sky, conserving energy while searching for prey.

Evening: Winding Down

The evening, as the day draws to a close, is a time of transition and preparation for the night. Birds exhibit increased activity during this period, focusing on the last opportunities for foraging before darkness sets in. This activity is crucial for building up their reserves to sustain them through the night.

As the sun sets, the ambient light changes, casting a unique glow over the landscape. Birds take advantage of this period to intensify their foraging efforts. This is a wonderful time to observe their feeding techniques and preferences as they search for insects, berries, or seeds.

Additionally, evening is a time when birds return to their roosting sites. Observing the dynamics and interactions at these communal roosts can offer valuable insights into their social structure and hierarchy. Certain species, such as crows or starlings, may exhibit elaborate displays and vocalizations during this time, contributing to the overall spectacle.

Bird Behavior Throughout the Day

Bird behavior is a fascinating subject that varies throughout the day, driven by a multitude of factors such as light, temperature, food availability, and social interactions. Understanding these behavioral patterns enhances the birdwatching experience and allows enthusiasts to appreciate the complexity of avian lives.

Morning Behavior: A Symphony of Activity

Mornings are a bustling time in the bird kingdom. As the sun begins to rise, birds are infused with energy and enthusiasm. Their songs fill the air, creating a symphony of sound that announces the start of a new day. This phenomenon, known as the dawn chorus, is a culmination of various birds staking their territorial claims and communicating with potential mates.

During the morning, birds are primarily focused on foraging and feeding. They scour the landscape for insects, fruits, seeds, and other sources of sustenance. This is a critical period for replenishing energy reserves after the overnight fast. Birdwatchers can observe different feeding strategies, from ground-feeding to aerial insect-catching, providing insights into their dietary preferences and hunting techniques.

Additionally, morning is a time of social interaction and courtship. Many birds engage in displays to attract mates and establish breeding territories. Intricate dances, vocalizations, and vibrant plumage displays are common sights, showcasing the beauty and diversity of avian courtship rituals.

Midday Behavior: Seeking Respite

As the day progresses and temperatures rise, birds seek respite from the heat. Midday represents a period of reduced activity, with many birds retreating to shady spots to escape the scorching sun. Rest becomes a priority, allowing them to conserve energy for the more active periods in the morning and late afternoon.

During midday, birds engage in grooming and preening activities. This serves to maintain their feathers in optimal condition, essential for flight and insulation. It's also a time for birds to repair any damage to their plumage, ensuring they remain in prime shape for the challenges of survival.

Social interactions continue but at a subdued pace. Birds may engage in brief bouts of communication, reaffirming their social bonds within the flock or their individual territories. However, the intensity of these interactions is notably lower compared to the earlier hours.

Afternoon Behavior: Preparing for the Night

Late afternoons witness a resurgence of activity among birds. They venture out to forage and feed, preparing for the upcoming night. This period is crucial for building energy reserves to sustain them during the hours of darkness when foraging becomes challenging.

Birds engaged in preening activities are a common sight during late afternoons. Ensuring their feathers are in optimal condition is essential for survival, providing effective insulation against the cool night air. Bathing activities may also take place, aiding in hygiene and feather maintenance.

Furthermore, late afternoons are an opportune time to observe birds in flight. Many species take to the skies, displaying their aerial prowess and agility. The fading light of the evening often creates captivating silhouettes, accentuating their flight patterns and showcasing the elegance with which they navigate the skies.

Evening Behavior: Transitioning to Rest

As the day transitions into the evening, birds begin their preparations for the night ahead. Foraging efforts intensify, focusing on gathering sufficient food to last through the night. The atmosphere becomes a hive of activity as birds make the most of the remaining daylight.

Birds return to their roosting sites, congregating in communal areas where they will spend the night. These roosts can range from trees to cliffs or even urban structures. Observing the dynamics at these roosting sites offers insights into their social structure and interactions within the flock.

In the lead-up to nightfall, some birds engage in specific rituals. These may include vocalizations, displays, or group formations. These behaviors are thought to strengthen social bonds within the flock and reinforce the sense of unity and safety as they settle in for the night.

Recording Weather Patterns

Birdwatching is a deeply enriching hobby, allowing individuals to connect with nature and the diverse wildlife that inhabits our surroundings. Observing and recording birds in your garden opens a window into the lives of these fascinating creatures. To truly understand their behavior and habits, it's crucial to record not just their actions but also the environmental factors that influence them. One of the fundamental aspects often overlooked is recording weather patterns during observations.

The correlation between weather and bird behavior is profound. Birds, like any other creature, respond to changing weather conditions in various ways. Bright, sunny days often lead to increased bird activity, with birds readily visible, foraging extensively, and engaging in social interactions. The sunlight provides optimal visibility, enabling them to efficiently find food and interact with their surroundings.

Conversely, rainy or stormy days significantly alter bird behavior. Birds tend to seek shelter during adverse weather, reducing their visibility and activity levels. They may hide in trees or bushes to stay dry, minimizing their foraging and socializing. The change in behavior during inclement weather underscores the adaptability and survival instincts of birds.

Wind, too, plays a crucial role in bird behavior. Different species of birds adjust their flight patterns and feeding habits based on wind conditions. For instance, soaring birds often utilize wind currents to aid their flight, conserving energy during long-distance travel. Ground-feeding birds, on the other hand, may struggle to forage efficiently in strong gusts, altering their feeding routines.

Long-term Observations: Seasonal Changes

One of the most rewarding aspects of birdwatching is the opportunity for long-term observations. Beyond the joy of a single encounter lies the ability to observe birds and their environment throughout different seasons, uncovering the subtle changes and patterns that characterize each phase of the year.

Spring: A Time of Renewal and Rebirth

As winter's chill recedes and days lengthen, the natural world awakens to the promise of spring. The arrival of this season brings a delightful surge of activity among the avian inhabitants of your garden. Migratory birds, returning from their winter sojourn, herald the onset of spring. Their cheerful songs fill the air, announcing the warmer days ahead.

For birdwatchers, spring is a time of excitement and anticipation. It marks the beginning of the breeding season, with birds establishing territories, building nests, and engaging in courtship rituals. The garden transforms into a bustling arena of vibrant plumage and musical notes as birds vie for mates and secure nesting spots.

Summer: Nurturing the Future Generation

With the arrival of summer, the focus of bird behavior shifts to the care and nurturing of their fledglings. Parent birds tirelessly forage to provide sustenance for their young, ensuring they grow strong and capable of flight. The once-hushed garden echoes with the hungry chirps and calls of fledglings eagerly awaiting their next meal.

Summer is a crucial period for observing the dynamics within bird families. The dedicated parenting efforts, the teaching moments as young birds learn to fly, and the constant feeding routines offer a glimpse into the resilience and dedication of these feathered parents. As fledglings take flight and gain independence, the garden witnesses a sense of accomplishment and growth.

Autumn: Preparing for Change

As the days shorten and temperatures gradually drop, autumn sets in, signifying a transition in the birdwatching calendar. Some birds, both resident and migratory, start their preparations for the upcoming winter. Flocks of migratory birds gather, fueling up on food to embark on their long journey to warmer climes.

Observing this pre-migration behavior offers unique insights into the strategies birds employ to ensure a successful migration. Documenting the gathering of these avian travelers, their feeding frenzies, and their synchronized departures enriches our understanding of migration patterns and the instinctual drive for survival.

Winter: Adapting to Adversity

Winter poses significant challenges for birds as they contend with colder temperatures and limited food availability. The garden may seem quieter during this season, with fewer bird species present. Those that stay must employ clever foraging strategies and energy-conserving behaviors to survive.

Birdwatchers can observe the resilient efforts of birds during winter, such as their adaptations to find food sources, their reliance on bird feeders, and their communal roosting tendencies for warmth. Documenting these adaptive behaviors underscores the remarkable resilience and resourcefulness of birds in the face of adversity.

PART 3

IDENTIFYING BIRDS IN YOUR GARDEN

| CHAPTER 1 |
BASIC BIRD ANATOMY

Birds are fascinating creatures, renowned for their diverse species, remarkable adaptations, and intricate anatomy. In this chapter, we delve into the intricacies of avian physiology, exploring the various parts that make up a bird's body and understanding the importance of plumage. Additionally, we explore how birds communicate, highlighting the significance of their vocalizations and body language. Finally, we discuss molt and its crucial role in bird identification.

Head to Tail: Bird Parts Defined

The avian anatomy, from head to tail, is a masterpiece of evolution, finely crafted over millions of years to equip birds with the necessary tools for survival and adaptation to their respective habitats. Understanding the various components of a bird's anatomy is crucial for appreciating their behavior, ecological roles, and evolutionary origins.

Beak

The beak, or bill, is a prominent and versatile feature of a bird's anatomy. It serves a multitude of functions, reflecting the bird's diet and habitat. The shape and size of the beak are directly related to the bird's feeding behavior and the types of food it consumes. For instance, a raptor's sharp, hooked beak is designed for tearing into flesh, while a finch's small, conical beak is ideal for cracking seeds.

In addition to feeding, a bird's beak also plays a vital role in preening, nest building, and other essential activities. The structure of the beak varies greatly across different species, showcasing the incredible diversity of avian adaptations.

Head

The head of a bird houses several critical components, including the brain, eyes, ears, and mouth. The eyes are typically located on the sides of the head, granting birds a wide field of vision. This binocular vision is particularly advantageous for predators, allowing them to accurately judge distances and hunt prey.

The ears, though less visible, are highly developed and contribute to a bird's keen sense of hearing. While some birds have ear openings concealed behind feathers, others have more prominent ear structures, depending on their ecological needs.

Neck

The neck is a flexible and essential part of a bird's anatomy, enabling a wide range of movements. Birds use their necks for various activities, including grooming, feeding, and courtship displays. Long-necked birds, like herons and cranes, use their extended necks to forage in aquatic environments, showcasing how different bird species have evolved to utilize this feature uniquely.

Torso

The torso encompasses the chest and abdomen, housing vital organs such as the heart, lungs, liver, and digestive system. The respiratory system of birds is particularly efficient, allowing them to extract oxygen from the air at high altitudes during flight. Air sacs, an integral part of the avian respiratory system, play a crucial role in this efficient gas exchange process.

Wings

Wings are the hallmark feature of birds, providing them with the ability to fly. The structure of a bird's wing is a marvel of natural engineering, consisting of intricate arrangements of bones, muscles, and feathers. The wings vary in shape and size depending on the species and their particular mode of flight. Raptors possess broad, powerful wings, enabling soaring and gliding, while hummingbirds have small, rapid-beating wings suited for agile, hovering flight.

Legs and Feet

A bird's legs and feet are specialized according to its lifestyle and habitat. Birds that spend a significant amount of time perching, like songbirds, have strong feet with well-developed claws for gripping branches. Waterfowl and wading birds have long legs, ideal for wading in marshes and shallow waters. Raptors have sharp talons for capturing prey, underscoring the diversity of adaptations within the avian leg and foot structure.

Tail

The tail of a bird serves multiple purposes, contributing to balance during flight and aiding in steering. Different species possess tails of varying lengths and shapes, each adapted to their unique needs. For example, a swallow's deeply forked tail enhances its aerial agility, enabling rapid changes in direction during flight. Woodpeckers utilize their stiff tail feathers as a prop while climbing tree trunks.

The Significance of Plumage

Plumage, the collective term for a bird's feathers, is a remarkable feature that serves a multitude of purposes beyond the mere aesthetic. It is a testament to the evolutionary journey that birds have undertaken, showcasing adaptation, survival strategies, and intricate biological mechanisms. Plumage plays a crucial role in a bird's life, impacting their ability to fly, stay warm, and communicate with others of their kind.

Feathers

Feathers are specialized structures made primarily of keratin, a protein found in human hair and nails as well. They are unique to birds and are crucial for their ability to fly and maintain their body temperature. Feathers are categorized into different types based on their function. Contour feathers, for instance, provide the shape and contour to a bird's body, aiding in aerodynamic flight. Down feathers, on the other hand, are soft and fluffy, providing insulation and warmth.

Coloration

The colors and patterns of a bird's plumage serve a myriad of functions, influencing their interactions with the environment and other members of their species. Camouflage, a form of protective coloration, allows birds to blend seamlessly into their surroundings, evading predators or stalking prey. Conversely, bright and vibrant plumage is often associated with attracting mates during the breeding season. These colors also indicate a bird's overall health and genetic fitness, a key factor in mate selection.

Molting

Molting is a vital process in a bird's life cycle. It involves the shedding and replacement of feathers, ensuring the plumage remains in good condition. Feathers wear out over time due to exposure to the elements and the demands of flight. Molting allows birds to rejuvenate their plumage, ensuring optimal function and efficiency. It is also during molting that birds may transition between different plumages, such as the shift from breeding to non-breeding plumage.

Specialized Adaptations

Birds have evolved unique plumage adaptations to suit their specific needs and habitats. For example, penguins, which spend a significant portion of their lives in the water, have dense, waterproof feathers that keep them warm and dry while swimming. In contrast, desert-dwelling birds might have feathers with reflective properties to help reflect sunlight and keep them cool in the scorching heat.

How Birds Communicate

Birds are masters of communication, employing a diverse array of vocalizations, body language, dances, and visual displays to convey information within their species and to interact with other wildlife. Communication is a fundamental aspect of their lives, playing pivotal roles in mating, defending territory, warning of danger, and coordinating group activities.

Vocalizations

Vocalizations are perhaps the most recognizable and widely studied form of avian communication. The melodies, chirps, calls, and songs of birds resonate through forests, fields, and urban landscapes, filling the air with their unique voices.

Each bird species possesses a distinct repertoire of vocalizations tailored to its specific needs and social structure. These vocalizations serve various purposes:

Mate Attraction

One of the primary functions of bird vocalizations is mate attraction. Males often sing or call to establish their presence and fitness to potential mates. The quality and complexity of a male's song can signal his genetic fitness and suitability as a partner. For example, the intricate and melodious songs of male songbirds like robins and nightingales are designed to captivate females.

Territory Defense

Birds use vocalizations to defend their territories. This is particularly common during the breeding season when competition for nesting sites and resources is fierce. Species like the Northern Mockingbird are notorious for their repertoire of songs and calls used to deter intruders and signal ownership of a specific territory.

Warning Calls

Alarm calls are another crucial aspect of avian vocalizations. Birds emit sharp, distinctive calls to alert their flock or neighboring birds to the presence of predators. The concept of "mobbing" is a fascinating phenomenon where smaller birds will vocally harass and even physically attack a predator to drive it away.

Coordinated Activities

In flocking birds, vocalizations play a role in coordinating group movements. Birds like geese and pigeons use specific calls to synchronize flight patterns, maintain formation, and communicate changes in direction.

Body Language

Birds are not limited to vocalizations when it comes to communication; they also employ body language to convey information. A bird's posture, movements, and gestures can be highly expressive.

Aggression and Submission

Body language is often used to convey aggression or submission within a group or during territorial disputes. For instance, when two birds square off in a territorial dispute, they may puff up their feathers, spread their wings, and engage in a ritualized dance to establish dominance. Conversely, submissive postures involve lowering the head, folding the wings, and making oneself appear smaller to avoid confrontation.

Mating Displays

Courtship displays involve elaborate body language. Birds like peacocks engage in flamboyant courtship dances to attract a mate. The male spreads its iridescent tail feathers into a magnificent fan, arches its neck, and struts in a choreographed performance designed to captivate females.

Parent-Offspring Interactions

Parent birds and their chicks also communicate through body language. Parents may use specific movements or postures to encourage their young to eat, shelter, or explore their surroundings. Chicks, in turn, may employ begging postures to signal hunger.

Predator Avoidance

Birds are attuned to the body language of potential predators. They can interpret the actions and movements of other animals and react accordingly. For instance, the sight of a stalking cat or a circling raptor will trigger alarm behaviors in a flock of smaller birds.

Dances and Displays

Some birds take communication to an even more visually striking level through dances and displays. These behaviors are often associated with courtship rituals and are used to attract mates or establish dominance.

Peacock's Dance

The peacock's dance is among the most famous avian displays. The male peacock fans out its iridescent tail feathers raises them like a magnificent fan, and struts in a highly synchronized dance. This visually stunning display is intended to impress and attract a female peahen.

Birds of Paradise

Birds of paradise, found in New Guinea, are renowned for their elaborate courtship displays. Each species has a unique dance that involves vibrant plumage, intricate movements, and vocalizations. These displays are a testament to the lengths birds go to in order to secure a mate.

Great Crested Grebe's Ritual

The great crested grebe, a water bird, engages in a mesmerizing courtship display. Two grebes face each other on the water, raise their bodies out of the water in a synchronous dance, and engage in rapid head-shaking movements. These rituals cement their bond as a breeding pair.

Flamingo Group Displays

Flamingos, known for their pink plumage and distinctive long legs, engage in synchronized group displays. These displays involve synchronized head-flagging, wing-flapping, and vocalizations. Group displays reinforce social bonds and help in pair formation.

Visual Signals

Birds also communicate through visual signals, often involving the display of colorful patches, feathers, or ornaments. These signals can convey various messages, such as readiness to mate, dominance, or submission.

Throat Patches

Many bird species have brightly colored patches on their throats, which they can puff up or display to signal aggression or readiness to defend territory. This behavior is particularly notable in hummingbirds, where males engage in fierce aerial battles to establish dominance.

Head Crests

Crested birds, such as cockatoos and herons, have ornate head crests that can be raised or lowered. Raising the crest can signal excitement or agitation while lowering it can indicate submission or relaxation.

Courtship Ornaments

Male birds often develop specialized ornaments during the breeding season to attract females. These ornaments can include colorful plumage, facial wattles, or distinctive head crests. For example, male northern cardinals sport brilliant red plumage, which they display to court potential mates.

Tail Displays

The tail feathers of birds can be highly expressive. For instance, the tail-fanning behavior of male wild turkeys during courtship displays showcases their intricate feather patterns to females.

Molt and its Importance in Identification (ID)

The process of molt, the periodic shedding and replacement of feathers, is a fundamental aspect of a bird's life cycle. It is a complex biological phenomenon with profound implications for bird identification, as it provides valuable insights into a bird's age, sex, and health.

Molt Cycles

Birds go through distinct molt cycles throughout their lives, with the two primary types being pre-basic molt (post-breeding molt) and pre-alternate molt (pre-breeding molt). Understanding these cycles is crucial for bird identification.

Pre-Basic Molt

Pre-basic molt occurs after the breeding season, typically in late summer or early autumn. During this molt, birds shed their worn feathers and replace them with fresh ones. This molt is essential for maintaining the integrity of feathers, which can become damaged or worn out during the rigors of nesting and caring for young.

Pre-Alternate Molt

Pre-alternate molt takes place before the breeding season, usually in late winter or early spring. It allows birds to acquire their vibrant breeding plumage, which is often more colorful and distinctive than their non-breeding plumage. This molt is especially critical for attracting mates during the breeding season.

Molt Sequences

The order in which feathers are molted can vary among species. Some birds undergo a simultaneous molt, where they replace all their feathers at once. Others undergo a sequential molt, where feathers are replaced in a specific sequence. The molt sequence is often consistent within a species and can be a valuable tool for identifying birds.

1. **Primary Feathers**: The primary feathers, located at the tip of the wing, are molted and replaced in a predictable sequence. Understanding this sequence allows birdwatchers to identify a bird's age and sex, as well as distinguish between juveniles and adults.
2. **Body Feathers**: Body feathers also follow specific molt patterns, and the timing and sequence of body feather molt can provide additional information about a bird's age and health.

Juvenile Plumage

Many young birds have distinctive plumage that differs from adult birds. This juvenile plumage is often duller and less colorful, providing better camouflage and protection as the young birds learn to fend for themselves. As they mature and go through molts, their plumage gradually transforms into the more vibrant colors of adulthood. Identifying juvenile plumage is critical for accurate bird identification and tracking population demographics.

Seasonal Changes

Molt is influenced by the changing seasons and is often synchronized with factors such as food availability, temperature, and day length. Birds may molt more actively during periods of abundant food to support the energy-intensive process of feather replacement. Understanding the seasonal patterns of molt can aid in predicting when and where certain bird species will molt, enhancing birdwatching experiences and contributing to research efforts.

| CHAPTER 2 |

BIRD SONGS
AND CALLS

One of the greatest joys of welcoming birds into your garden is the symphony of sights and sounds their presence creates. Listening to the diverse vocalizations of different avian species adds auditory beauty and interest to your landscape. Tuning into distinguishing bird calls also aids greatly in identifying visitors even when they flit quickly out of view. Developing your ears to discern the unique songs and calls of birds takes some practice, but doing so will enrich your birding experience and help prevent misidentification. This chapter covers tips on focusing your listening skills, common vocalizations to learn, recording bird sounds for later analysis, and understanding the contexts and timing when birds call and sing. Soon, your garden will come alive with identifiable birdsong.

Listening Before Looking

When trying to identify a bird, the most helpful clues are often auditory rather than visual. Colorful plumage fades into the shadows or foliage; swift flight makes distinguishing features blur; dense vegetation obscures shape – vision can fail. But a clearly heard song or call rings true no matter where the bird is. Training your ears to recognize avian vocalizations before your eyes even locate the singer will give you an identification advantage.

Start by simply closing your eyes when you hear an unknown birdcall – this eliminates distraction and focuses listening intently. Cup hands around ears to amplify and locate the sound. Pick out distinguishing features like speed, pitch, tone, volume, trills, buzzes or whistles. Note any repeating patterns or unique phrases. Listen for changes as the bird moves or when other birds respond. Allow the sound to create a clear mental impression before opening your eyes to look. Having the auditory clues in mind while watching the bird will make its visual cues more recognizable.

With practice, you can learn to readily identify common garden birds by sound alone, like the rapid "chik-a-dee-dee" call of a chickadee, the whistled "drink-your-teeeeaaa" song of an Eastern towhee, or the buzzy electrical hum of a hummingbird. Listening carefully first prepares you to look at a bird with identifying features already in mind. So, train ears before eyes to make birdwatching rewarding for both senses.

Common Bird Calls to Recognize

Every bird species uses particular calls to communicate needs like warning of danger, claiming territory, attracting mates, bonding with flock mates, begging for food, and more. Calls are innate rather than learned. Here are some key common garden bird calls to learn:

Chickadee: The black-capped chickadee's namesake "chick-a-dee-dee" call rings out high, loud and clear in woods and yards. More "dees" mean higher alarm levels. Often, the first call is learned by ear.

Northern cardinal: A loud, metallic "chip!" emanates from brush piles and hedges as Northern cardinals call out contact notes and warnings. Both genders make a sweetly whistled song of short phrases.

Mourning dove: The mournful cooing of this common dove carries through woods and backyards, a peaceful "ooAH oo, oo oo-oo-oo-oo." Easily mistaken for an owl.

Red-winged blackbird: From atop cattails and reeds, male red-wings call "kon-ka-ree" with visceral urgency, the syllables blurring together. A softer, querulous "churr" follows.

Killdeer: The "kill-deer, kill-deer" call, sounding like its name, rings out stridently as these ground-nesting plovers try to lure predators away from nests. Listen for the shrill quality.

Woodpecker: Woodpeckers make an attention-grabbing, sharp, loud "Pik!" drill-like call, along with drumming on trees. Great spotted woodpeckers make a ceasing call of loud ringing "qui-qui-qui."

Nuthatch: From high up in pines, the red-breasted nuthatch's nasal, tin-horn-like "yank-yank" call rings out stridently. The white-breasted nuthatch makes a softer, nasal "yenk-yenk."

Chipping sparrow: An evenly paced rhythmic repetition of high-pitched "tsip" notes identifies the modest chipping sparrow. The call persists as the bird hops along, feeding.

Eastern screech owl: A haunting, quavering "whinny-like" descending whine identifies this small owl. Often called the "lonesome train" call.

Great horned owl: Look for the classic "hoo-hoooo-hoo-hoo" deep booming call, sometimes mistaken for a mourning dove on steroids. Male and female calls are different pitches.

Eastern phoebe: A distinct "FEE-bee" call, louder and more emphatic than chickadees, rings out above streams and under eaves where these flycatchers nest.

Blue jay: The harsh, nasal "jay! jay!" shriek of the blue jay stands out sharply amid other woodland calls, sometimes sounding like a hawk.

American crow: A loud, gratingly harsh "caw-caw-caw" rings out as crows communicate across territories. Regional dialects exist in crow calls.

Tufted titmouse: A dropping, see-saw whistle called "peter-peter" emanates from treetops where titmice are active. The call is often repeated in a series.

House finch: Bright, bouncy warbling emanates from finch flocks, interspersed with "wit" or "vitt" contact calls among the musical jumble.

American robin: Cheery caroling of the robin greets spring and continues through summer, a string of exuberant whistled phrases "cheerily, cheer up, cheerio."

Song sparrow: A melodic jumble of chirps, trills and whistles comes from these vocal ground dwellers. Their song often ends on a distinctive downward trill.

Common raven: A deep, reverberating "cronk-cronk" call rings out as these large corvids soar overhead. Sometimes they make a quavery, laughing "wonk-wonk."

When Birds Sing: Behavior and Timing

Not all bird vocalizations serve the same purpose. Calls tend to be shorter and relate to messages like alarms or warnings. But singing is longer, more melodic and complex, associated with courtship and individual recognition. Different species also prefer certain times of day and seasons for increased singing and calling:

Dawn Chorus: Most songbirds sing vigorously at dawn to claim territory and attract mates. Males serenade loudest in the breeding season. Listen for the feathered chorus around sunrise.

Night singers: Owls, nighthawks, and insect-eating bats vocalize on the wing after dark. Spring peepers and other amphibians chorus at night.

Migration: Long migratory flights occur at night when the air is calmer. So, nocturnal flight calls from warblers, thrushes and others are common seasonal sounds.

Seasonal changes: Longer daylight and breeding urges stimulate birdsong starting in late winter through spring. Males sing to mark nest sites and court females before breeding.

Social contact: Flocking birds like chickadees and titmice maintain contact and locate food with frequent calls all day long. Feeding area chatter aids identification.

Territorial defense: Resident birds sing frequently to claim areas, using unique songs to identify themselves to rivals. Birds on migration sing less.

Mating communication: paired birds may vocalize to relay location, food source, or progress feeding young. Duets help keep pairs together.

Mimicry: Some birds incorporate other species' sounds into their own repertoire for deception or expanding vocal range. Northern mockingbirds are famous mimics.

With experience, you will recognize who is likely calling or singing based on behavior context, time, and season. Identifying the purpose behind a vocalization also helps discern the species. Whether it's an early riser's dawn song, social call, or dusk-to-dawn night bird, bird sounds all contribute to the symphony of your nature soundscape.

CHAPTER 3

SEASONAL BIRDS AND MIGRATION PATTERNS

One of the greatest wonders of welcoming birds into your garden is observing the seasonal ebb and flow of species passing through. The bird life changes dramatically with each turning of the seasons; as migrants arrive and depart, temperatures shift, foods change and migration instincts take hold. Developing an understanding of how birds move with the seasons, which species come and go in your region, how weather influences migration, and yearly arrival and departure timing will help you anticipate and observe the parade. Soon, you will come to know what Birdsong announces each new season at hand.

Predicting Arrival and Departure

Birds follow natural cycles tuned over thousands of years, but modern records help us track those seasonal movements and arrive at average migration timing. Keeping yearly notes on your garden's lineup can refine predictions even more. Peak arrival times in spring and prime departure periods in fall follow similar patterns year to year.

Spring

The first rumblings of the coming spring are sounded by resident mating pairs and early nesters like cardinals, chickadees, titmice and jays. February into March, bring woodpeckers, nuthatches and other short-distance migrants back from southern wintering grounds. True harbingers of spring come in April and May when neotropical migrants making epic journeys arrive – bright warblers, vireos, swallows, orioles, tanagers and more. April onward, waves of visitors continue to return and pass through each week.

Summer

June brings peak breeding season, with males singing vigorously to attract mates and birds busily building nests. By July, parents have clutches of demanding, hungry nestlings. Fledglings appear in August, clumsy on the wing but doted on by adults. Resident populations are at their height, with migrants now nesting across the region. The greatest bird diversity and abundance occurs in summer when all species converge.

Fall

The first hints of autumn's approach come as shorebirds gather in flocks heading south, and hummingbirds grow scarce at feeders by late August. September brings southbound warbler waves, along with flycatchers, buntings, grosbeaks and others joining the exodus. By late October, juncos and sparrows arrive from the northland to overwinter. Golden-crowned kinglets and yellow-rumped warblers now grace the quiet winter landscape.

Winter

December and January host the lowest overall diversity as fair-weather migrants vacate. Resilient permanent residents like chickadees adapt to winter's challenges. Birds band together more in wintering flocks and frequent feeders. By February, the first rumblings of mating songs emerge, and the cycle begins anew. Cold months contain quiet wonders for devoted birders to observe.

Keeping detailed notes each year on first arrival and last departure dates, as well as peak abundance, will uncover patterns for your location. Weather and climate changes may shift timing, but knowing averages helps anticipate seasonal occurrences. Soon, you will know spring is coming when bluebirds return to nest boxes, winter is waning when horned larks sing over fields, and fall has arrived when white-throated sparrows return to scratch in leaf litter.

The Mysteries of Migration

One of the most mystifying marvels of the avian world is how relatively tiny songbirds transform into globe-trotting travelers each spring and fall. Weighing just ounces, they can fly astonishing distances of thousands of miles between breeding and wintering grounds. The Arctic tern makes a 50,000-mile round trip yearly between pole to pole. Tiny hummingbirds brave a nonstop 600-mile journey across the Gulf of Mexico. Even "short distance" neotropical migrants travel a few thousand miles each way. And many species make the trip multiple times in a lifetime.

Scientists are still working to unravel the amazing physiological changes that enable long-distance migration. Fat stores fuel the flights, nearly doubling birds' weights before migratory journeys. Sharp vision adapted for night navigation keeps birds oriented. Internal compasses based on the earth's magnetic field guide direction. Sophisticated location and mapping abilities let migrants return to the exact same breeding and wintering sites yearly. And an ingrained clock synced to seasonal changes tells them when to travel. We still don't fully comprehend their navigational tools and triggers.

Equally astounding is the actual mechanics of travel. Flapping tens of thousands of wingbeats takes tremendous energy, yet birds can cover 30-100 miles in a single night's flight. Some species prefer traveling in short hops, stopping over to rest and refuel, while others make nonstop marathons over oceans and deserts. Alternating bursts of powered flying with periods of gliding rest different muscle groups. Birds plan routes to take advantage of helpful tailwinds and avoid overwater perils when possible. There is safety in numbers during migration, and intricate timing keeps populations in sync. The whole process speaks to the amazing resilience of birds.

As you welcome traveling birds to your yard, contemplate the mighty distances and obstacles overcome just to arrive. Even familiar robins may have migrated thousands of miles between your yards. Nurture needed resources for these globe trotters to help speed them on their way.

How Weather Affects Bird Movement

The peak timing of spring and fall migration depends heavily on weather patterns each year. Birds wait for optimum conditions before undertaking risky, long journeys. Cold temperatures, storms, and headwinds all deter departure, while warm, calm, clear weather motivates migration. Birds may arrive weeks earlier or later than average based on seasonal weather variations.

In spring, birds generally wait for warm southerly winds to assist northbound travel and rain-free conditions. Ideal conditions fuel rapid progress. But storms like late spring nor'easters can majorly delay migrants. Birds forced into headwinds and cold weather may retreat back south until suitable conditions return or even perish in extremes.

Fall migration timing follows similar patterns. Migrants wait until fronts move through and any storms clear. Wind direction is key – northerly winds provide tailwinds to aid southbound journeys. Hot, dry, late summers can motivate earlier travel to take advantage of the weather while abundant food lasts. But early cold snaps and winter storms arriving when birds are still in transit can be devastating.

Keep an eye on weather forecasts during peak migration times. Alerts for storms, winds, precipitation, and temperature swings can help you anticipate impacts on bird movements. Checking radar imagery for the density of arrivals or departures on favorable nights can also indicate migration activity. Note weather conditions each day alongside first arrival and last departure dates in your birding journals to spot connections.

Birds to Watch for In Each Season

Anticipating yearly cycles will help you identify birds passing through your garden with the changing seasons. These are some signature species to enjoy:

Spring

- Early Nesters: cardinals, chickadees, titmice, robins, mourning doves, blue jays
- Returning Woodpeckers: red-bellied, downy, hairy, flickers
- Swallows: purple martin, tree, barn, cliff, bank swallows
- Hummingbirds back from Mexico and Central America
- Vibrant neotropical Warblers: yellow, yellow-rumped, palm, pine, prairie
- Musical Thrushes: hermit, wood, Swainson's, gray-cheeked
- Sparrows and Juncos are moving north to breed
- Tanagers, grosbeaks, buntings and orioles pass-through

Summer

- Nesting activity at a high pitch with residents and migrants
- Fledglings of every species learning to fly and feed
- Warblers, thrushes, and flycatchers are now summer nesting residents
- Scarlet tanagers gleaming from treetops
- Indigo buntings singing from open perches
- Orchard and Baltimore's orioles snacking on oranges and berries
- Ruby-throated hummingbirds buzzing through gardens

Fall

- Large flocks of blackbirds and grackles gather to migrate
- Warblers, vireos, and flycatchers passing southward again
- Sparrows and juncos arrive from the north to overwinter
- Rusty fox sparrows scratching through autumn leaves
- Winter wren's ringing song emerging from shaded thickets
- Sharp-shinned and Cooper's hawks passing through on migration
- Greater and lesser yellowlegs often stop to refuel at ponds
- Fieldfare and other winter finches and siskins are arriving

Winter

- Foraging flocks of chickadees, titmice, nuthatches and woodpeckers
- Rowdy American robins join flocks, eating berries insatiably
- Cedar waxwings descend on trees laden with fruit, often startlingly tame
- Bright yellow goldfinches and juncos are frequenting feeders daily
- Red-breasted nuthatches call raucously from treetops
- Raptors like bald eagles, snowy owls and rough-legged hawks hunt open fields
- Elegant northern shrikes may stop over on your fence line to hunt

Attuning yourself to the rhythms of bird migration will make their passages through your yard all the more wondrous. Recording arrival and departure dates each year will add to both your bird identification skills and your appreciation for the persistence of migrating birds. Soon, you will find that the movements of wild birds give a constantly refreshing vitality to your garden throughout the seasons.

| CHAPTER 4 |
FIELD GUIDE UTILIZATION

Birdwatching is a fascinating hobby that allows enthusiasts to connect with nature and gain a deeper understanding of the avian world. To embark on this captivating journey, it is crucial to equip oneself with the right tools and knowledge. A reliable field guide is an indispensable companion for any birdwatcher, serving as a window into the intricate realm of avian diversity. In this chapter, we delve into the profound importance of a good field guide, explore the nuances of choosing between electronic and print guides, highlight notable field guides to consider, and discuss the art of making annotations and keeping records.

Electronic vs. Print Guides

In today's digital age, birdwatchers have a choice between traditional print field guides and their electronic counterparts, typically accessible via smartphones, tablets, or specialized e-readers. Both formats have their merits and considerations, and the preference for one over the other often depends on individual preferences, circumstances, and the specific demands of the birdwatching excursion.

Print guides, the longstanding cornerstone of birdwatching, provide a tactile and aesthetically pleasing experience. The satisfaction derived from flipping through the pages, encountering vibrant illustrations and comprehensive information, is a unique aspect of print guides. Birdwatchers revel in the sensory experience, feeling a more profound connection with the natural world as they leaf through the pages filled with depictions of diverse avian species.

Another advantage of print guides is their autonomy from technology and their dependence on power sources. Whether in remote, off-the-grid locations or areas with limited access to electricity, a print guide remains a reliable and accessible source of information. There's a sense of tradition associated with print guides, as they have been the primary tool for bird identification for generations, and this traditional appeal is often cherished by birdwatchers.

On the other hand, electronic guides offer a modern and tech-savvy approach to birdwatching. They are lightweight, portable, and can store an extensive collection of bird species. Electronic guides often feature search functionalities, making it quick and convenient to pinpoint specific birds based on their attributes. Additionally, they can incorporate multimedia elements, including photographs, audio recordings of bird songs, and videos, providing a multimedia learning experience.

One significant advantage of electronic guides is their capacity to receive regular updates. As new research emerges and taxonomic classifications evolve, electronic guides can seamlessly incorporate these updates, ensuring that birdwatchers have access to the most current and accurate information. Moreover, the search and filter options available in electronic guides allow for swift access to desired information, aiding in efficient bird identification.

However, electronic guides do come with a set of challenges. The need for a power source, typically a charged battery, is a critical requirement for accessing an electronic guide. Birdwatchers must consider battery life and carry power backup solutions to ensure continuous access to the guide, especially during extended outings. Furthermore, screen glare in bright outdoor settings can hinder visibility and readability, posing a challenge for some users.

Notable Field Guides to Consider

1. "The Sibley Guide to Birds" by David Allen Sibley

"The Sibley Guide to Birds" by David Allen Sibley stands as a pinnacle in the realm of field guides. Its reputation is anchored in the author's meticulous illustrations and comprehensive coverage of North American birds. The guide showcases remarkable attention to detail, capturing each bird's distinct features with astonishing accuracy. Sibley's artistry brings the birds to life, making it a favorite among both amateur and experienced birdwatchers.

One of the standout features of this guide is its unique layout. Birds are often depicted in various poses, reflecting their typical behaviors and postures. This layout aids in identification, as it mirrors how the bird might appear in the field. Additionally, accompanying the illustrations are extensive text descriptions, providing insights into behavior, habitat, vocalizations, and regional variations. These details offer a holistic understanding of each species.

Beyond the illustrations and descriptions, "The Sibley Guide to Birds" includes range maps, making it a valuable tool for understanding the distribution of bird species. This guide's comprehensiveness and user-friendly design make it a must-have for any serious birdwatcher, whether a beginner or a seasoned enthusiast.

2. "The Peterson Field Guide to Birds of North America" by Roger Tory Peterson

Roger Tory Peterson, a pioneer in the field of field guides, introduced the "Peterson Field Guide to Birds of North America." This guide has earned a timeless reputation for its user-friendly design and clear, informative illustrations. Peterson's system of identification, which utilizes arrows and pointers to highlight key features, revolutionized birdwatching and set a standard for subsequent field guides.

The guide's illustrations are distinctive and focus on aiding rapid identification, presenting variations in plumage, age, and gender. Additionally, the range maps included in this guide are highly detailed, offering crucial information about a bird's distribution throughout North America.

One notable aspect of the "Peterson Field Guide" is its emphasis on field marks, the unique characteristics that differentiate one bird species from another. This focus on distinct features empowers birdwatchers to make quick and accurate identifications while in the field. Overall, this guide's clarity, accessibility, and emphasis on crucial identification features make it an essential tool for birdwatchers.

3. "Collins Bird Guide" by Lars Svensson, Killian Mullarney, and Dan Zetterström

The "Collins Bird Guide" is a widely acclaimed field guide, especially cherished by birdwatchers in Europe. The guide's strength lies in its accurate and lifelike illustrations, making it an indispensable resource for bird identification across the European continent.

The illustrations in this guide are not only comprehensive but also artistically engaging. Each species is depicted in various postures and angles, aiding in a thorough understanding of its appearance and behavior. Additionally, the guide offers detailed descriptions, maps, and even hints for distinguishing between similar species, further enhancing its utility.

A unique feature of the "Collins Bird Guide" is its inclusion of information on subspecies, a valuable resource for birdwatchers interested in taxonomy and variations within a species. This guide's comprehensive coverage, coupled with its focus on illustrating variations and subspecies, makes it an essential companion for birdwatchers exploring the rich avian life of Europe.

4. "Kaufman Field Guide to Birds of North America" by Kenn Kaufman

Kenn Kaufman's "Field Guide to Birds of North America" is a preferred choice for birdwatchers, especially those starting their birding journey. The guide's simplicity and emphasis on essential identification features make it ideal for beginners.

The illustrations in this guide are clear and concise, emphasizing the distinctive characteristics of each species. The illustrations are accompanied by straightforward, to-the-point text, facilitating a quick grasp of the bird's key features and behaviors. Additionally, the guide includes range maps, aiding in understanding a bird's distribution across North America.

What sets the "Kaufman Field Guide" apart is its compact size and lightweight design, making it easily portable for field excursions. The guide's emphasis on simplicity, ease of use, and compactness caters to the needs of beginners and casual birdwatchers, providing a solid foundation for their birding endeavors.

5. "Birds of Europe" by Lars Jonsson

Lars Jonsson's "Birds of Europe" is an exemplary guide specifically tailored for European birdwatchers. The guide is highly regarded for its artistic and evocative illustrations, adding an aesthetic dimension to the birdwatching experience.

Jonsson's artistic prowess shines through in the illustrations, capturing not only the physical features but also the spirit of each bird. The guide features birds in their natural habitats, providing a glimpse into their world. Accompanying the illustrations are detailed descriptions and maps, presenting a comprehensive view of the avian fauna of Europe.

A noteworthy aspect of "Birds of Europe" is its focus on habitat and behavior. The guide delves into the ecological context of each bird, shedding light on their preferred habitats, feeding behaviors, and nesting patterns. This ecological perspective enriches the birdwatching experience, allowing enthusiasts to appreciate birds within the broader natural landscape.

RARE BIRDS AND SPOTTING TECHNIQUES

In the world of birdwatching, there is perhaps nothing more exhilarating than the sight of a rare bird gracing your garden with its presence. These elusive and uncommon species can captivate the heart of any dedicated birder, offering a unique thrill that sets them apart from the common avian visitors. This chapter explores the art of recognizing rare visitors, understanding their habitats, connecting with fellow birders, and the crucial aspect of reporting and documentation.

Recognizing Rare Visitors

The world of birdwatching is a realm of wonder and excitement where enthusiasts find solace in the quiet observance of our feathered friends. Among the many joys birdwatching offers, spotting a rare visitor is an unparalleled thrill. A rare bird, in this context, is an avian species that infrequently graces a particular region, habitat, or ecosystem. It could be a migratory bird on an unusual route, a vagrant straying far from its typical territory, or even a species whose population is rapidly declining, making every sighting a momentous event.

The Importance of Recognition

The first step towards the joy of identifying rare birds lies in proper recognition. Birdwatchers, both novice and experienced, must cultivate an understanding of the distinctive characteristics that set these uncommon species apart. This includes studying the unique features of their plumage, beaks, feet, and tails, which are often vital clues in identification.

Field guides and comprehensive reference books dedicated to birds are essential tools for recognizing these visitors. The literature provides a wealth of information, including vivid illustrations, behavioral traits, preferred habitats, and geographic distributions. Carrying a trusted field guide specific to your region is akin to having a reliable companion during your birdwatching excursions.

Observation and Patience

Observation is the cornerstone of recognizing rare birds. A keen eye and a patient demeanor are vital qualities for a birder. Rare birds are elusive; they do not readily expose themselves to casual observation. They often camouflage within their surroundings, making their detection a delightful challenge.

To enhance your observation skills, take the time to immerse yourself in the natural world. Study the behavior of common birds to better understand deviations that might indicate the presence of a rare species. Note unusual movements, distinct calls, or anything out of the ordinary that might hint at a rare visitor in your vicinity.

Networking and Information Sharing

Birdwatching is a communal endeavor, and the collective knowledge of a community is an invaluable asset in recognizing rare birds. Networking with fellow birders, both locally and globally, can greatly amplify your chances of identifying and spotting uncommon species.

Joining birding groups, whether in your neighborhood or online, opens up a treasure trove of shared experiences. These groups often organize birdwatching trips, outings, and workshops, providing ample opportunities to learn from others and witness rare bird sightings. Sharing your own experiences and sightings also contributes to the collective knowledge base, fostering a collaborative spirit among bird enthusiasts.

Utilizing Technology for Identification

In the contemporary era, technology has significantly enriched the birdwatching experience. Smartphone applications and online platforms designed for bird identification have become valuable resources. These applications use artificial intelligence and vast databases to identify birds based on images or audio recordings. Utilizing these technologies can aid in rapidly identifying and confirming rare bird sightings.

Habitats of Uncommon Species

Uncommon bird species often have very specific habitat requirements that allow them to survive and thrive. These habitats may be rare or declining, putting extra conservation pressure on the species that depend on them. Understanding what makes these habitats special and how different birds utilize them is key to protecting biodiversity.

Many uncommon birds rely on mature forests, which provide critical resources but are threatened by logging and development. The ivory-billed woodpecker, for example, is thought to be extinct primarily due to loss of old-growth southern swamplands. They require large tracts of unbroken forest with dense hardwood trees. Their specialized habitat allows them to find food sources like beetle larvae under bark and evade predators. Other mature forest specialists, like the spotted owl, nest in tree cavities and forage amongst dense canopy cover. Fragmentation of these habitats leaves birds more vulnerable to weather, predators, and competition.

Wetlands are another threatened habitat that provides irreplaceable ecosystem services. Marshes, swamps, and bogs have been drained for agriculture and urbanization despite supporting specialized birds like bitterns and rails. These species are masters at navigating through dense vegetation. Their compressed bodies allow bitterns to walk stealthily with little movement to startle prey. Rails have elongate toes that provide balance and prevent sinking into muddy soils. Wetland loss hits these uniquely adapted birds hard.

Some birds rely on natural disturbances to create their preferred habitats. Woodpeckers, like the black-backed woodpecker, specialize in burned mature forests. Fires create an abundance of wood-boring beetle larvae for them to prey on. But fire suppression policies mean these natural post-fire habitats are becoming rare. Prescribed burns and protection from naturally ignited fires are needed to maintain habitats for this species.

Grassland habitats have also faced massive declines. Birds like the mountain plover and burrowing owl require shortgrass prairies. These birds avoid trees, nest on the ground, and have camouflaged plumage to avoid aerial predation. But native prairies have been converted to agriculture or lost to succession. Protecting remaining patches and using grazing or fire to prevent tree encroachment is vital.

Even harsh arctic and desert habitats host specialized birds, like the sandhill crane and common raven. The long legs, neck, and beak of sandhill cranes allow them to forage in wetlands for crustaceans, insects, and small vertebrates. Ravens are intelligent generalists who cache food and use communal roosting in deserts. Protecting the uniqueness of these extreme environments preserves important biodiversity.

Island birds are also very vulnerable due to their isolation and endemic status. Hawaiian honeycreepers evolved spectacular beak diversity to utilize specific food sources in forest habitats. However, these habitats have been decimated by ranching, agriculture, logging, and invasive species. Protecting their remaining native forests is crucial.

Protecting uncommon bird species means protecting the distinctiveness of their habitats. It requires understanding natural disturbance regimes, geographic isolation, vegetation composition, soil types, and food availability. Bird species and their habitats have evolved in unison over millennia. If we wish to preserve biodiversity, we must maintain the unique environmental circumstances that allow it to flourish in all its splendid variation.

Networking with Fellow Birders

Birdwatching is a hobby that extends beyond the mere act of observing and identifying birds. It's a passion that connects individuals with a shared love for avian creatures and the natural world. Networking with fellow birders not only enhances the joy of birdwatching but also adds a significant educational and social dimension to the hobby. Through mutual interaction, exchange of knowledge, and collaboration, birdwatchers can deepen their understanding of birds, refine their identification skills, contribute to scientific research, and promote conservation efforts.

Community and Camaraderie

One of the most enriching aspects of networking with fellow birders is the sense of community and camaraderie it fosters. Birdwatchers often form bonds based on their shared passion, creating a supportive network of individuals who understand and appreciate the unique thrill that birdwatching provides. This sense of belonging encourages new enthusiasts to join the fold, ensuring the growth and sustainability of the birdwatching community.

Birding clubs and local birdwatching groups are at the forefront of this sense of community. These organizations often organize regular outings, meetings, workshops, and events that facilitate interactions among members. Through these gatherings, birdwatchers share their experiences, discuss sightings, and exchange tips and techniques, creating an environment conducive to learning and growth.

Learning and Knowledge Sharing

Networking with fellow birders provides ample opportunities for learning and knowledge sharing. Birdwatchers come from diverse backgrounds and possess a wealth of knowledge about different bird species, habitats, behaviors, and identification techniques. Engaging with this diverse group allows you to tap into a vast reservoir of experience and expertise.

Experienced birders often act as mentors, guiding newcomers and sharing their insights and expertise. They may offer advice on where to spot specific bird species, share tips on identifying challenging birds, and provide recommendations on equipment and field guides. The collective wisdom of the birding community becomes a valuable resource for honing your birdwatching skills.

Collaborative Birdwatching Expeditions

Collaborative birdwatching expeditions epitomize the spirit of networking in the birding community. These outings involve groups of birders joining forces to explore different habitats and observe birds collectively. Such expeditions not only enhance the chances of spotting rare and elusive species but also create a platform for collaborative learning and sharing experiences.

During these expeditions, birders often designate roles and responsibilities, ensuring a systematic and organized approach to birdwatching. Some may focus on spotting, others on identification, and some on documenting the sightings. This division of labor enhances efficiency and improves the overall birding experience for everyone involved.

Support and Encouragement

The birding community offers a significant source of support and encouragement to its members. For beginners, venturing into the vast world of birdwatching can be overwhelming, but having a network of experienced birders provides a safety net of guidance and encouragement.

Experienced birders often motivate beginners to keep pursuing their passion, offering advice on overcoming challenges, sharing their own early experiences, and suggesting strategies to improve. This encouragement fosters a nurturing environment, empowering birders to persist, learn, and evolve in their birdwatching journey.

Reporting and Documentation

Reporting and documentation are fundamental components of responsible birdwatching. It goes beyond the excitement of a sighting; it involves recording valuable information that contributes to scientific understanding and conservation efforts. By meticulously documenting your observations and sharing them through appropriate channels, you become an active participant in the world of ornithology and environmental conservation.

The Importance of Accurate Reporting

Accurate reporting of bird sightings is crucial for several reasons. Firstly, it helps maintain a reliable record of bird populations, behaviors, and distribution. This data can be analyzed to detect trends, study bird migration patterns, and assess the impact of various factors on bird populations.

Secondly, accurate reporting aids in species conservation. Rare or endangered species can be identified, and appropriate conservation measures can be implemented based on reported sightings and habitat information. Moreover, researchers rely on this data to make informed decisions regarding conservation strategies and policies.

How to Document Sightings Effectively

Documenting bird sightings effectively involves a systematic and comprehensive approach. Start by noting down the date, time, and specific location of the sighting. Provide details about the bird's behavior, its physical characteristics, and any distinguishing features. Include information about its habitat and the environmental conditions at the time of the sighting.

Photography and/or sketches play a vital role in documenting bird sightings. Clear photographs capturing the bird's plumage, beak shape, and other identifying features can be immensely helpful for accurate identification and verification. If possible, record the bird's calls or songs, as these auditory cues can aid in identification and add valuable data to your observation.

Reporting Platforms and Databases

In the digital age, reporting bird sightings has become more accessible and efficient. Numerous platforms and databases cater to birdwatchers, allowing them to submit their observations and contribute to scientific research and conservation efforts. One prominent platform is eBird, which offers a user-friendly interface for birders to report their sightings and access a vast database of avian information.

When using reporting platforms, ensure that you provide accurate and detailed information about your sightings. The data you submit is valuable to researchers, conservationists, and fellow birdwatchers, shaping our understanding of bird populations and their behaviors.

Contribution to Scientific Research

By reporting your bird sightings and contributing to databases, you actively participate in scientific research. Ornithologists and researchers often rely on citizen science data for their studies. Your observations can help answer questions about bird distribution, behavior changes, and responses to environmental factors.

Researchers may also use the data to track the effects of climate change on bird populations, assess the success of conservation efforts, or determine the impact of urbanization on avian habitats. Through your contributions, you become a vital part of the scientific process, advancing our knowledge of birds and their ecosystems.

Networking with fellow birders and engaging in responsible reporting and documentation significantly enhance the overall birdwatching experience. The community aspect of birdwatching provides a sense of belonging and an environment of shared enthusiasm. Collaborating with other birders amplifies learning, supports newcomers, and fosters a sense of camaraderie that enriches the hobby.

PART 4

HOW TO PHOTOGRAPH BIRDS IN YOUR GARDEN

| CHAPTER 1 |

CHOOSING THE RIGHT CAMERA AND LENS

Capturing beautiful photographs of birds in your own backyard requires having the right camera equipment. When it comes to photographing our feathered friends, the two most important pieces of gear are the camera body and the lenses. There are several factors to consider when selecting a camera and lens that will meet your needs for bird photography. In this chapter, we will explore the advantages and disadvantages of DSLR and mirrorless camera bodies, the different types of lenses best suited for birding, and accessories like tripods and flash that can help you achieve tack-sharp images.

Camera Types: DSLR vs. Mirrorless

The first major decision is choosing between a DSLR (digital single lens reflex) camera or a mirrorless camera. Both options have their benefits and drawbacks when it comes to photographing fast-moving subjects like birds.

DSLR Cameras

A DSLR camera has been the go-to choice for most serious photographers over the past couple of decades. DSLR cameras have proven themselves to be very fast, responsive, and reliable for capturing action. They use a complex mirror mechanism that allows you to visually compose your image through the lens via an optical viewfinder. When you press the shutter button, the mirror flips up, the shutter opens to expose the image sensor, and then everything resets for the next shot. This tried-and-true DSLR technology results in a very short lag time between shots since no image processing is required in the viewfinder. The optical viewfinder also gives you a bright, crisp image even in challenging lighting conditions. These traits make DSLR cameras well-suited for bird photography.

DSLRs give you the flexibility to choose from a huge range of interchangeable lenses specific to your photographic needs. Telephoto prime lenses with long focal lengths are essential tools for birders to capture detailed shots of birds from a distance. With a wide selection of telephoto lenses made by Canon, Nikon, Sigma, Tamron, and others, there are many excellent lens options for DSLR users.

The main drawbacks of DSLRs compared to mirrorless cameras are their larger size, heavier weight, and louder operation due to the moving mirror. This can make them more difficult to handhold for extended periods and challenging to use inconspicuously when you want to sneak up on skittish birds. However, the fast performance and optical viewfinders of DSLRs still make them very capable cameras for bird photography.

Top DSLR Recommendations for Birding:

- Canon EOS 90D
- Nikon D500
- Pentax K-3 III

Mirrorless Cameras

Mirrorless cameras have exploded in popularity over the last decade as an alternative to the long-dominant DSLR design. Mirrorless cameras forego the optical viewfinder and complex mirror mechanism in favor of an electronic viewfinder and a more digitally focused capture process. Because there is no mirror to flip up, light passes directly to the image sensor at all times. This allows mirrorless cameras to offer features like real-time exposure preview and face/eye detection autofocus while viewing the scene on the LCD or electronic viewfinder.

The simpler mechanical design of mirrorless cameras results in them being smaller, lighter and much quieter during operation compared to most DSLRs. This makes them better suited to up-close birding since they are less obtrusive. You can move them quickly to track a flying bird and shoot without scaring away the rest of the flock. Mirrorless cameras also have very fast shooting speeds, often capable of 10+ frames per second in burst mode. This helps you capture the perfect pose as a bird rapidly switches positions.

Many of the latest mirrorless cameras also meet or exceed the autofocus capabilities of equivalent DSLRs. Focus modes like eye detection are extremely useful for getting tack-sharp shots of birds. Mirrorless cameras are quickly catching up to DSLRs for shooting action and will likely surpass them in the next few years as the technology improves.

The smaller size of mirrorless cameras does mean using smaller image sensors in most consumer and prosumer models compared to DSLRs. This can negatively impact low-light performance. However, the newest full-frame mirrorless models compete directly with high-end DSLRs in terms of image quality. Mirrorless cameras are also compatible with adapters to allow the use of lenses from DSLR mounts. This expands the possibilities of lenses available to aspiring bird photographers using a mirrorless system.

Top Mirrorless Recommendations for Birding:

- Sony a7 IV
- Fujifilm X-T4
- Olympus OM-D E-M1X

Lens Choices for Bird Photography

The lenses you choose will have a huge impact on the quality of images you can capture of neighborhood birds. Bird photography requires specialized lenses that offer long focal lengths to get close to the action. The ideal lenses also need fast aperture settings to isolate the subject against a blurred background and let in enough light for fast shutter speeds.

Here are the main lens characteristics to evaluate when shopping for bird photography:

Focal Length - This determines how closely you can frame the bird. Look for telephoto lenses in the 200-600mm range.

Aperture - Faster lenses (lower f/numbers like f/2.8 or f/4) provide better background blurring and performance in low light.

Stabilization - Vibration reduction technology is essential for handholding long lenses.

Autofocus - Fast, silent AF motors allow you to track moving birds.

There are two routes you can take in choosing a lens setup for birding:

1. Telephoto Zoom Lens - Convenient all-in-one option allowing you to cover a range of focal lengths
2. Prime Lens - Single fixed focal length lens that typically offers wider aperture

Next, we will do a deeper dive into the pros and cons of zoom lenses versus prime lenses for photographing birds.

Telephoto Zoom Lenses

Zoom lenses make bird photography much more flexible by providing a range of focal lengths in one lens. Bird behavior can be unpredictable, so having the ability to frame shots more tightly or pull back for context is a major advantage of zooms. This lets you react quickly as the opportunities change rather than having to switch lenses back and forth.

Zoom lenses designed specifically for sports and wildlife photography are the best options for birders. These telephoto zooms offer long ranges like 150-600mm or 200-500mm in a single lens. This provides enough magnification to capture intimate portraits or frame small birds tightly when they are farther away.

The trade-off is that telephoto zoom lenses have narrower maximum apertures like f/5.6 or f/6.3, meaning they don't perform as well in low light. They also tend to focus a bit slower than prime lenses. However, technological improvements have made the latest versions of lenses, like the Sigma 150-600mm F5-6.3 DG OS HSM Sports, very capable for bird photography.

Recommended Telephoto Zoom Lenses for Birding:

*   Tamron 150-600mm f/5-6.3 Di VC USD G2
*   Sigma 150-600mm f/5-6.3 DG OS HSM Sports
*   Nikon 200-500mm f/5.6E ED VR

Prime Lenses

Prime lenses have a fixed focal length rather than zooming. While this means you have to physically move closer or farther from your subject to frame your shots, primes offer advantages in image quality and performance. They have wider maximum apertures, which translates to superior low-light capabilities and blurred backgrounds. Prime lenses are also lighter, smaller, and less expensive than comparable telephoto zooms.

A major reason professional bird photographers often use prime lenses is that they allow wider apertures like f/2.8 or f/4. This gives several stops better light gathering compared to a zoom lens at f/5.6 or f/6.3. If you want to shoot handheld in the golden hours around sunrise or sunset, the speed boost of a fast prime lens makes it possible.

The ideal pairing for bird photography is using a short telephoto prime lens like a 400mm f/2.8 for superior optical performance and wide aperture, along with a teleconverter like a 1.4x or 2x extender to increase the magnification. This provides the versatility to shoot at 400mm, 560mm, or 800mm, depending on your distance from the bird. Prime lenses retain excellent sharpness and speed even with teleconverters.

Top Prime Lens Picks for Birding:

- Nikon 400mm f/2.8 FL ED VR
- Canon 600mm f/4L IS III
- Sigma 500mm f/4 DG OS HSM

Lens Features to Look For:

- Fast maximum aperture (f/2.8, f/4)
- Teleconverter compatibility
- Weather sealing
- Fluorite lens elements
- Advanced coatings (reduces flare and ghosting)

Ultimately, the choice between zoom or prime lenses comes down to budget, shooting style, and what compromises you are willing to make. Zoom lenses provide more flexibility and convenience, while fast telephoto primes offer superior performance in challenging lighting. Weigh your options carefully before investing. Renting lenses to try them out first can be worthwhile before making a big purchase.

Tripods and Stability Accessories

A tripod or monopod is required to take full advantage of your expensive camera equipment for bird photography. The stabilization allows you to shoot at slower shutter speeds and maximizes the resolution possible from your lenses. Trying to handhold heavy telephoto lenses typically necessitates shooting at faster shutter speeds to avoid camera shakes and blurry images. But with solid support, you can get back the sharp focus at much slower shutter speeds and lower ISOs for cleaner images.

Tripods

Tripods provide the most stable base for bird photography with long telephoto lenses. They allow very slow shutter speeds down to a full second or longer while still maintaining crisp focus. Look for tripods that extend tall enough for you to shoot comfortably without crouching. The substrate the legs are positioned on will also affect stability. Setting up on pavement or a deck typically provides a more vibration-free foundation than grass or dirt.

A gimbal head on the tripod allows smoother tracking of birds in flight by providing two axes of rotation. Tripods with built-in leveling bases are also extremely helpful for bird photography. This lets you quickly achieve a level horizon even on uneven ground.

Recommended tripods for bird photography:

- Gitzo Systematic Series 3
- Really Right Stuff TVC-34L Versa Series 3
- Oben CT-3531 Carbon Fiber Tripod

Monopods

Monopods offer an excellent compromise between handholding and tripods when mobility and weight are a priority. Using a long, sturdy monopod allows you to take advantage of the telephoto reach and fast shutter speeds without carrying a full tripod setup. Monopods provide stabilization while remaining lightweight and fast to reposition as birds move around. This makes them ideal for tracking skittish birds on the go.

Look for monopods that extend to about eye level for the most stability. Five-section models collapse down small for easy transport. Be sure to get one rated to support the weight of your lens/camera combination. Using the monopod with a wrist strap provides additional support when panning and tracking motion.

Top monopod picks for birding:

- Benro Mach3 9C Carbon Fiber Monopod
- Vanguard VEO 2 265CB Carbon Fiber Monopod
- Manfrotto Compact Light Aluminum 5-Section Monopod

Portable Camera Supports

In addition to tripods and monopods, there are a few smaller devices to help provide stability for bird photography while handholding telephoto lenses:

- Lens collar - Allows you to grip the lens rather than the camera for better balance
- Lens sling - Camera sling that attaches to the lens tripod foot for added support
- Shoulder/chest brace - Provides an additional contact point, minimizing shake
- Elbow pads - Cushioning to make handholding large lenses more comfortable

Any additional support like these accessories makes a big difference in sharpness when using longer focal lengths without a monopod or tripod. They allow you to shoot at slightly slower shutter speeds while remaining steady.

The Role of Flash in Bird Photography

While photographing birds outdoors, most shots will be captured using natural light only. However, an addition like fill flash can be used judiciously to improve results when bright sunlight creates high-contrast lighting situations.

Natural light is beautifully diffused on overcast days, making it easier to photograph birds among the shadows and highlights of a complex scene. But direct sunshine often means intensely bright backgrounds and dark shadow areas that exceed the camera's dynamic range. The camera will either expose the highlights and leave the subject underexposed or expose the subject and blow out the bright areas.

In these situations, using fill flash is an excellent solution to balance out the contrast and allow properly exposed images. The small amount of light reaching the shaded side of the bird from the flash results in a more evenly lit photo. This prevents the subject from being rendered too dark when exposed to a bright background. The flash can either be attached via a hot shoe on the camera body, held off-camera, or built into the camera if you have a model with that capability, like the Fujifilm X-T4.

Basic Steps for Using Fill Flash:

1. Set the camera to Aperture Priority mode
2. Choose an aperture that provides the desired background blur
3. Set ISO based on ambient light levels (typically ISO 400 or lower)
4. Let the camera select the shutter speed
5. Turn on the flash and set flash exposure compensation to -1 or -2 stops
6. Compose a shot and fire off a few test shots to check the exposure
7. Adjust flash power as needed for natural-looking illumination of the subject

A couple of key settings to watch when balancing flash with ambient light are the shutter speed and aperture:

- Shutter speed controls ambient light exposure. Keep shutter speed in the 1/200-1/400s range to avoid motion blur when handholding.
- The aperture controls flash exposure on the subject. Use an aperture like f/5.6 or wider to allow more flash illumination and background separation.

Using high-speed sync (if available on your flash unit) eliminates the limits on shutter speed, so you can continue shooting wide open with flash at faster speeds.

Off-camera flash, diffusers, and reflectors:

For greater control over the intensity, direction, and quality of light, you can use off-camera flash. This takes the flash off the hot shoe and positions it anywhere you choose using a cord or wireless trigger system. Side lighting from off-camera flash creates a more dimensional look compared to flat on-camera flash.

Diffusers and small reflectors are useful additions when using flash. Diffusers soften the harsh light emitted from the small flash head for a more flattering look. Reflectors allow you to bounce and redirect the light towards a shaded area on your subject. This opens up many possibilities for providing pleasing illumination even in deep shadow conditions.

Getting the most out of flash for bird photography requires practice and experience. But the stunning results you can achieve in situations with extreme dynamic range make it a valuable tool. Pay attention to the color temperature and quality of the light when balancing flash with natural light. With care taken to look natural, fill flash is a sure way to improve your bird portraits in sunny conditions.

A camera with high-speed burst shooting capability is mandatory for capturing wing motion and sudden movements. For rapidly approaching or passing birds, burst mode helps you nail the ideal moment. Fast autofocus tracking performance is also critical to keeping pace with a moving bird and maintaining focus.

Lenses with super-telephoto reach in the 400mm or longer range get you close enough for frame-filling images. A wide aperture setting like f/2.8 or f/4 maximizes the amount of light available and enables the blurring of the background into a creamy bokeh. Tripods, monopods, and other support accessories allow shooting at lower ISO and slower shutter speeds for the best possible quality.

DSLRs and mirrorless cameras now both offer compelling options for serious bird photography. Look for models with advanced autofocus, burst speeds of 10 fps or better, and a high-resolution sensor in either format. Mirrorless cameras have advantages in live view preview, silent operation, and often smaller/lighter overall systems. But DSLRs still excel at optical viewfinders and responsiveness for the following actions.

On the lens side, telephoto zooms and fast primes each have distinct strengths and weaknesses. Zooms offer unmatched flexibility at the cost of narrower apertures and larger/heavier builds. Primes boast superior low-light performance and optical quality in a smaller package. Many bird specialists own both types to experience the benefits of each for different scenarios.

With the amazing lens technology available today from third-party manufacturers like Sigma and Tamron, you can assemble professional-level gear for reasonable prices. Don't underestimate the value of upgrading your equipment if you feel limited by current limitations. The leap in image quality and photographic opportunities from pro gear over entry-level equipment is massive.

Investing in robust, specialized bird photography tools paves the way for truly phenomenal photos from your own backyard. We wish you the best of luck finding your ideal setup for unlocking newfound creativity and capturing inspiring bird images!

CHAPTER 2

LIGHTING AND COMPOSITION TECHNIQUES

In the world of photography, capturing the beauty and essence of birds in your garden is a rewarding and challenging endeavor. It involves not only understanding your camera and its settings but also mastering the art of composition and making the most of available lighting conditions.

Understanding the Golden Hours

The golden hours refer to the periods shortly after sunrise and before sunset when the quality of natural light produces rich, warm tones and long, dramatic shadows. This is considered the optimal time for photography, especially for capturing wildlife like birds in their natural habitats.

In the golden hours, the sun is low in the sky, producing a softened raking light that enhances textures and colors. The low angle of the sunlight creates strong directional shadows that give depth and dimension to photographs. The warm color temperature of the light during sunrise and sunset also imparts a magical quality, and the extended shadows and golden light evoke a sense of drama and mood.

For bird photography, the golden hours are ideal for bringing out details like feathers and plumage. The soft lighting is also flattering for photographs and helps separate small birds from busy backgrounds. The shadows add depth and shape to give a 3D effect. And the overall golden glow can impart a timeless, nostalgic quality to bird portraits.

The duration of the golden hours varies but typically lasts around 40 minutes after sunrise and before sunset. This window is shorter in summer with longer days and longer in winter with shorter days. The golden light is not instant at sunrise or sunset either. It takes at least 10-15 minutes after sunrise or before sunset for the light to warm up and produce the signature golden tones.

So timing is important for effectively photographing birds during the golden hours. You want to anticipate and be set up and ready during the peak periods of magical light. Monitoring the weather forecast the day before and planning your shoot around the exact sunrise/sunset times will help maximize your chances. Apps and websites provide tools for determining exact sunrise and sunset times based on location.

Given the fleeting nature of the golden hours, preparation is key. Scout locations beforehand and know where the light will be falling and where you want to photograph from. Have your camera settings dialed in and your gear ready to go rather than fumbling at the last minute. Because the light transitions quickly, test shots are also important to check camera settings and make any adjustments to aperture, shutter speed, and ISO as needed.

The golden hours present ideal lighting conditions, but that warm directional light can also be used to create dramatic shadows and silhouettes, which brings us to our next topic...

Shadows and Silhouettes

While the soft frontal lighting of the golden hours is excellent for illuminating detail, side lighting from a low sun during the golden hour can produce strong shadows. And shadows can add visual interest and depth to bird photography composition.

Shadows help separate a bird from the background, almost like a natural vignette. Light raking from the side can cast shadows from a bird's body onto the ground or a nearby tree trunk. This provides separation and highlights the bird's shape. The shadow lends a sense of depth and layers to the composition. Lighting the bird but having shadow fall on the background helps the bird stand out, too.

Strong directional side lighting can also create rim light effects. If the sun hits a bird from behind at a side angle, it can outline the shape of the bird's body, feathers, and beak in light. This rim lighting effect provides separation and makes the details pop.

Low-side lighting can also create silhouettes. If the light source is directly behind the bird, exposing the bright background will render the bird a dark shape or silhouette. This can produce graphic, artistic compositions. Positioning a bird against a brightly lit sky at sunset captures its silhouette shape. Silhouettes work especially well for birds with distinctly recognizable shapes, like owls or flamingos. Side lighting that silhouettes a bird against golden hour light produces striking high-contrast images.

When intentionally photographing silhouettes and shadows, metering for the bright areas while letting the shadowed bird go dark is key. This often requires manual exposure settings or exposure compensation adjustments to override the camera's autoexposure. Aim to retain some highlight detail in the brighter areas to avoid a harsh look. But rendered properly, shadows and silhouettes leverage the directional golden hour lighting to bring added dimension and artistic flair.

Composing the Perfect Shot

Beyond ideal lighting, composing a pleasing and effective bird photograph requires careful consideration of various compositional elements and techniques.

Framing - Framing refers to what is included inside the boundaries of the photograph and how that was chosen. Tighter framing that isolates the bird as the main focal point versus wider framing that includes more of the context and environment can completely change the feel of the shot. Consider if you want to capture a portrait framing of just the bird or a wider environmental framing showing it in its habitat.

Orientation - Vertical or horizontal orientation is an important framing choice that can emphasize different aspects. Vertical framing may better capture a tall standing bird, while horizontal framing works better for a wide scene or a bird in flight.

Perspective - Perspective relates to the camera's distance from the subject and angle relative to it. Photographing a bird from eye level provides a different perspective than photographing it from above or below. Each perspective provides a different viewpoint. Lower perspectives tend to give the subject prominence, while higher perspectives can diminish and look down on a subject.

Leading Lines - Compositional lines that point to or lead towards the main subject help direct attention. These can be naturally occurring elements like tree branches, forest streams, fence posts, or other linear aspects of the environment. Positioning a bird at the end of leading lines draws the viewer's eye.

Rule of Thirds - Placing key elements like the bird according to the imaginary grid of the rule of thirds (dividing the frame into horizontal and vertical thirds) often results in a pleasing, balanced composition. Putting the bird off-center according to the rule of thirds points rather than placing it centered.

Negative Space - Negative space refers to the open areas around the main subject. Having some negative space around a bird can provide separation from the background and draw attention to it. But, too much empty space may make the composition feel unbalanced and choppy.

Depth - Using strategically placed foreground and midground elements can add depth. Placing a bird in front of background elements like foliage or branches helps give depth and dimension to the scene.

Patterns and Textures - Composing the bird against backdrops with interesting colors, patterns, or textures helps accentuate it. Photographing a vivid red bird against green foliage or a textured stone wall boosts visual appeal.

Simplification - Keeping the composition simple by eliminating distracting elements helps keep the viewer's eye on the main subject bird. Some selective framing and perspectives can simplify. Post-processing can also be used to crop away or subdue distracting background elements.

With practice and experimentation, bird photography composition can become more intuitive over time. Observing the way professional photos frame bird subjects provides helpful examples to learn from, too.

Depth of Field and Background Choices

Two additional technical considerations that significantly impact the look of bird photographs are depth of field and choice of background.

Depth of field refers to the area in focus from front to back. A shallow depth of field has just the main focus point sharp and blurs the foreground and background areas. This is achieved with wide apertures like f/2.8-f/4. Meanwhile, a larger depth of field keeps more of the scene from front to back in focus. Smaller aperture settings like f/8-f/16 produce a larger depth of field.

For bird photography, there are merits to both approaches. Using a shallow depth of field by widening the aperture can beautifully blur out distracting backgrounds, isolating the bird as the sole point of focus. But sometimes, you want to maintain details in the habitat the bird is photographed in. If so, stopping down for a larger depth of field can keep the bird and foreground/background elements all sharper.

The choice depends on the context and aim of each specific shot. Using aperture priority mode lets you easily adjust the aperture opening to control the depth of field. Autoexposure will select the shutter speed needed for each aperture chosen. Toggling between f/stops and evaluating results on the LCD screen lets you experiment to find the optimal depth of field.

The other key choice is selecting appropriate backgrounds. For portrait-style bird shots, choosing clean and non-distracting backgrounds simplifies the composition. A blurred background from a shallow depth of field can elegantly frame a bird. Natural backgrounds like green foliage, trees, grass or sky tend to complement bird subjects well. Avoid busy or cluttered settings.

But for environmental shots, embracing more complex natural settings that communicate habitat and context may be desirable. This requires picking backgrounds that enhance rather than detract. Any strong colors or patterns should complement, not compete with, the bird as the main focal point. A bright red feeder won't enhance a red cardinal, for example. Again, depth of field impacts whether environmental backgrounds appear sharp or blurred.

| CHAPTER 3 |
CAPTURING BIRDS
IN ACTION

Photographing birds in motion and in action poses unique challenges for any photographer. Birds are fast, agile creatures that can take flight in an instant and change direction abruptly. Their small size and ability to move quickly means photographing them requires patience, skill and specialized techniques to get good action shots. However, with some planning, knowledge of bird behavior, and camera settings tailored for speed, you can get stunning images of birds in your garden in full, dynamic motion.

Predicting Bird Movement

The key to capturing great bird action shots is being able to predict how and where they will move. This allows you to anticipate the shot and prepare your camera settings and positioning accordingly. Here are some tips for understanding and predicting bird movement:

Observe Flight Patterns

Pay close attention to the flight paths birds take through your garden. Make a note of any regular routes or habitual behaviors. Position yourself where you know birds frequently take off, land or fly through.

Follow Food Sources

Birds will go where the food is! Take note of bird feeders, fruiting trees/shrubs, or sources of insects that attract birds. Stake out these spots and wait for action.

Note Landing and Perching Sites

Birds have preferred perches and places they like to land. Watch where they hop to after eating at feeders or bathing in a fountain. Set up near these spots and be ready.

Consider Time of Day

Bird activity increases at certain times of day, notably in the early morning and hours before dusk. Schedule photo sessions during peak action times.

Watch for Disturbances

Anything that startles or disturbs birds will cause sudden movements like fast takeoffs or a change of direction. Be alert for cars, cats, other birds, etc., that might spook birds.

Patience is key. Spending time observing bird behaviors will help you learn their patterns and habits. Visit your garden regularly and take notes to identify peak activity levels at different times and locations. This will allow you to plan your photo shoots for the best chances of catching dynamic bird motions.

Using Baiting Techniques Ethically

One technique photographers use to attract birds and encourage interesting behaviors is called baiting. This involves placing food items, water sources, props or other enticements to draw birds to a staging area and keep them active there. However, baiting does raise some ethical concerns over disrupting natural behaviors and conditioning wild birds. Here are some tips for baiting birds ethically:

- Choose locations birds naturally frequent - Near bushes, feeders, fountains, etc. Avoid interfering with nests or habitats.

- Select foods birds are familiar with - Offer nuts, seeds, and fruit. Avoid anything unnatural that could cause harm if eaten.

- Scatter small amounts loosely on the ground - Don't pile up large concentrations of food.

- Use liquid bait like dripping or splashing water - It encourages motion without altering diets or nutrition.

- Limit sessions to short time periods - Long sessions can make birds dependent on baiting sites.

- Provide perches at varying heights and positions - Gives variety for different species and more pose options.

- Stop baiting if signs of distress are observed - such as injury between territorial birds competing for food.

The key is moderation. Bait birds sparingly with natural, nutritious foods in areas they frequent for short sessions. Avoid conditioning them to rely on artificial food sources. Be prepared to stop and intervene if birds display signs of distress from competing aggressively over bait. When used judiciously, baiting can give you great photographic opportunities without harming birds or their behaviors long-term.

Seasonal Patterns

Bird activity levels and behaviors will vary significantly throughout the year as seasons change. Here's an overview of seasons and what types of action shots you can capture during each one:

Spring - Prime time for courtship displays, mating dances, nest building and territorial conflicts. Capture birds displaying, chasing, and engaging in breeding or nesting behaviors.

Summer - Adults busy hunting for food for hatchlings often make frequent trips back to the nest. Young fledglings take their first flights. Try capturing birds in feeding flights, landing on nests and adolescent birds flapping awkwardly.

Autumn - Birds switch focus to fueling up for migration or overwintering. Increased foraging, fighting over food sources and migrating flocks present action shot opportunities.

Winter - Birds crowd limited food sources in cold weather and may bicker over access. Position near feeders to photograph jostling, posture displays and quick take-offs.

Knowing what behaviors are typical during different seasons will help you anticipate prime photo ops. Schedule your action shoot sessions when each season presents the peak activity you want to capture. Tracking seasonal patterns year after year will teach you when your garden birds are most lively and animated.

Tips for Quick Focus and Action Shots

Photographing fast-moving birds challenges even professional photographers. The tiny subjects are in near-constant motion and can change direction instantly. Capturing tack-sharp images takes specialized camera settings and techniques. Here are some tips for gear and settings to use:

- Choose a telephoto lens in the 400-800mm range - Gives tight zoom capability
- Select continuous focus and high-speed burst modes - Keeps refocusing on moving subjects and machine-gunning images
- Manual focus can be quicker than auto - Pre-focus on where birds will be and bypass focus hunting
- Use fast shutter speeds - Start at 1/1000s or higher to freeze motion
- Open up your aperture as wide as possible - Lets in more light for fast exposures
- Increase ISO to boost light sensitivity - Allows faster shutter speeds
- Pan smoothly to track erratic motions - Keeps bird centered as you move the camera
- Try panning - Match the subject's motion to deliberately blur the background
- Position yourself with a clean background - It is easier to isolate darting birds and get clean shots
- Follow through on action - Capture take-off, flight and landing to tell a story

With practice, you'll get a feel for what camera settings work best for your gear in the variable lighting conditions you encounter. Remember to continually review photos and adjust as needed. Proper preparation and settings will help you capture tack-sharp, thrilling images of the spirited, kinetic movements of garden birds.

CHAPTER 4

POST-PROCESSING AND SHARING YOUR PHOTOS

After spending hours in your garden capturing beautiful photos of birds, the next step is to import them to your computer and enhance them through post-processing. The editing process lets you transform your raw images into polished masterpieces that showcase the stunning colors and details of your avian subjects. Once your photos are edited to perfection, it's time to share them with the world through your photography portfolio, social media, contests and more.

In this chapter, we'll explore essential post-processing techniques for bird images, the best editing software options, creating an eye-catching bird photography portfolio, and strategies for sharing your work across various online platforms and communities. With proper processing and effective sharing, your backyard bird portraits can garner global acclaim.

Basic Editing Techniques

Post-processing allows you to enhance your photos through color correction, exposure adjustments, cropping, sharpening, noise reduction, and more. While professional-grade editing software like Adobe Photoshop and Lightroom provide endless options, you can dramatically improve your shots with just a few simple tweaks. Here are some basic editing techniques for bird photography:

- Cropping: One of the most useful editing tools is cropping your image to hone in on your subject and improve the composition. Tightly framing the bird often results in a stronger photo.

- Exposure: Adjusting exposure settings like highlights, shadows, whites and blacks helps recapture details lost in the original shot. Boost shadows to reveal the bird's plumage; lower highlights if they appear overexposed.

- Color correction: You can balance color tones and enhance vibrancy and saturation during post-processing. Many software tools let you adjust overall hue, brightness and individual color channels.

- Contrast: Increase contrast for a bold, dramatic look. Lower it to achieve a softer aesthetic. Contrast also accentuates plumage details.

- Sharpening: A touch of sharpening brings out texture and fine features in feathers and eyes. But be careful not to overdo it, as too much sharpening can appear unnatural.

- Noise reduction: Minimizing visual noise smooths unwanted graininess in high ISO shots. Use noise reduction sparingly at low sensitivities.

- Vignettes: Applying a vignette darkens photo corners to naturally draw the viewer's eye to the main subject. Subtle vignettes prevent distraction.

- Selective editing: Utilize selection tools to separately edit the bird and background. For example, you could brighten just the bird while increasing the contrast in the surroundings.

With practice and experimentation, you'll discover how to harness these editing functions to enhance your bird photography. Even basic adjustments make a noticeable difference.

Software Choices for Bird Photography

Advanced photographers use Adobe Photoshop and Lightroom for unparalleled editing capabilities, but there are other software options offering features tailored specifically for bird images.

Photoshop Elements - Adobe's budget-friendly alternative includes many core Photoshop tools like selections, layers, filters and adjustments. The Smart Tone option automatically fine-tunes lighting, color and contrast. Elements meet the needs of serious hobbyists.

Lightroom - Adobe's Lightroom was designed for workflow efficiency. Quickly sort, rate and organize photos into collections. Global and local editing tools like cropping, tone curves and noise reduction streamline enhancing large batches of bird images. Lightroom's raw processor renders stunning detail.

DxO PhotoLab - This software excels at scientific corrections and digital lens optimization. It automatically removes distortions, fringing, vignetting and artifacts. DxO analyzes RAW files using advanced demosaicing and noise reduction, coaxing out the utmost image quality. The local adjustment brushes give precise control.

ON1 Photo RAW - ON1 combines browsing, editing, layers, masking, presets and other tools in one slick interface. It's speedy and intuitive for applying effects to wildlife shots. The AI-powered masking selects subjects in one click. ON1 is subscription-free.

Topaz Labs - Topaz offers a suite of photo editing plug-ins focusing on areas like sharpness, noise reduction, color enhancement and contrast. Many plug-ins use AI technology for fast, automatic image improvement. Topaz simplifies the editing process.

Exposure X7 - Designed forRAW processing and layered editing, Exposure gives you creative control over colors, details, tones and contrast. It excels at recovering highlights, rich HDR effects, luminosity masking and haze removal - perfect for nature scenes.

Zoner Photo Studio - Affordable and user-friendly, Zoner contains efficient workflows for managing, editing and sharing image collections. Core tools include RAW processing, layers, local adjustments, presets and metadata management. There's even a clone tool.

PhotoDirector Ultra - CyberLink's editing software has a special Bird Mode that adds eye/feather enhancement, color pop, vignettes and other effects geared toward wildlife shots. The Refine Brush isolates and edits specific parts of a photo.

The beauty of software is the ability to download free trials and demos to discover the right editing programs for your style and proficiency level. Find tools providing all the filters, adjustments and features you need for superb bird images.

Creating a Portfolio

Nothing showcases your photographic abilities like a professional portfolio. Birding enthusiasts often judge a photographer's skills by the quality of images in their portfolio. Follow these tips to stand out:

Choose your best work - Be highly selective about the images you include. Only display your very best photos that demonstrate proficiency in composition, exposure, sharpness, lighting and other technical elements. About 10-20 extraordinary photos make more impact than 50 average ones.

Organize thematically - Group your photos into nature themes like birds in flight, birds in the garden, seasonal birdwatching, detailed close-ups, etc. Chapters and sections help viewers appreciate the full range of your work.

Get the print quality right - Portfolios may be presented online or offline. Print portfolios should use high-quality paper and professional lab printing to accurately convey colors, lighting and details. For online portfolios, export JPEG files at sufficiently large sizes (try 4800 pixels on the long edge), saving at 90%+ quality.

Choose a polished platform - Photography websites like SmugMug, Format, Zenfolio and Photoshelter allow you to create stunning online portfolios with your own domain name. Opt for clean, simple designs that let your photos take center stage. Display your name/logo elegantly.

Write useful captions - Every portfolio photo should have a meaningful caption identifying the bird species, location, relevant camera settings and other useful metadata. Captions provide context that engages viewers.

Update your work - Don't just set up your portfolio and forget about it. Add new photos periodically to feature your latest techniques and experiences. Rotate out older images. Stay active.

Promote your portfolio - Share your portfolio website address prominently on your email signature, bird photography social profiles and anywhere photographers may see it. The more exposure for your work, the better.

Your portfolio is the best tool for attracting clients, exhibitions, contests, fellow birders and new opportunities. Dedicate time to building a remarkable portfolio that astounds anyone who sees your beautiful backyard bird photographs.

Sharing on Social Media and Online Platforms

In addition to your professional portfolio website, social media provides endless possibilities for showcasing your bird photography to an engaged community of nature lovers. Let's explore some top sites for sharing your garden bird pics:

Instagram - This visual platform is ideal for bird photography feeds. Post stunning shots daily. Use relevant hashtags like #birds, #birdphotography, #yourcitybirds, etc. Engage with other bird accounts through likes and comments. Add location tags.

Facebook - Create a dedicated bird photography page to share photos, promote your work, announce exhibitions, and connect with fans. Post detailed captions explaining the story behind images. Share bird knowledge.

Flickr - The photo-centric Flickr community appreciates high-quality bird images. Join relevant groups like Birders, Nature Photography, Wildlife Photography, etc. Interact with members through discussions, favorites and comments.

500px - This network of professional photographers features curated galleries, photo critiques, challenges and more. Upload only your best bird images for a chance to be recognized. Use informative titles, keywords and descriptions.

Pinterest - Build eye-catching boards with your bird images to tap into Pinterest's massive audience. Boards could cover garden birds, birds in flight, owl photos, seasonal birds, etc. Link to your site.

Twitter - Engage fellow birders in conversations by tweeting your photos and observations using hashtags like #birdwatching. Retweet and comment on tweets from nature organizations, wildlife refuges, bird events and experts.

YouTube - Create a birding YouTube channel to share video content like timelapses of busy feeders, close-ups of birds bathing and singing, equipment tips, photography tutorials, or compiling your best still photos into videos or slideshows with music.

Local community - For direct local exposure, share your photos with neighborhood groups, gardening clubs, wildlife organizations, nature-themed businesses, master gardeners programs, conservation groups, parks and recreation offices, native plant nurseries, etc.

Photo contests - Enter your best backyard bird portraits into photo contests like Audubon's, National Wildlife Federation's, BirdPhotographers.net's contests, state/county fairs, camera club competitions, and more. Contests provide great exposure.

Online photo sites - Also post your photos to bird & nature-specific communities like Birdshare. Co, BirdPhotographers.net, NaturesPic, iNaturalist, WildSnap, ViewBug, etc. Engage with fellow bird photographers and fans.

The birding community is passionate about high-quality bird imagery. By actively sharing your photographs across social sites, contests and niche nature forums, your work can inspire people worldwide to connect with the feathered friends in their own backyards.

Mastering bird photography requires not just field techniques but also editing know-how and sharing expertise. Following the post-processing and distribution strategies in this chapter will take your backyard birding images to the next level. First, convert your RAW photos into striking masterpieces using editing tools that maximize color, sharpness, contrast and impact. Next, compile your best-edited images into a professional online portfolio that captivates nature lovers. Finally, promote your accomplishments by sharing your growing portfolio of beautiful backyard bird photos across birding communities, social media and online photography platforms.

The joy of photographing birds extends beyond the camera to the thrill of editing and presenting your remarkable images to engage and inspire. So continue honing your skills in the garden, at the computer and across the internet to become a widely recognized backyard bird photography sensation!

PART 5

DIY BIRD HOUSES, FEEDERS, AND BATHS

CHAPTER 1

BUILDING A BIRD HOUSE: STEP-BY-STEP GUIDE

Birdwatching has been a cherished hobby for many enthusiasts, and creating a haven for our feathered friends is a delightful way to invite them into our outdoor spaces. A birdhouse is a vital component of any bird-friendly garden, providing shelter and a safe environment for birds to rest and nest. In this chapter, we will delve into the intricate process of building a birdhouse from scratch, offering a comprehensive step-by-step guide for a successful DIY project.

Choosing Materials

Choosing the right materials is the foundation of a durable and welcoming birdhouse. The longevity and functionality of your birdhouse heavily depend on the quality and suitability of the materials used. Here's a detailed exploration of materials for your birdhouse:

1. **Wood Selection**: Begin by selecting appropriate wood for your birdhouse. Cedar, redwood, and pine are popular choices due to their durability and natural resistance to decay. Avoid pressure-treated wood, as the chemicals used can be harmful to birds.

2. **Thickness and Durability**: Opt for wood with a thickness of at least 3/4 inch to ensure stability and durability. Thicker wood will provide insulation against weather conditions and protect the birds better.

3. **Non-Toxic Paints and Sealants**: If you decide to paint your birdhouse, choose non-toxic, water-based paints that won't harm the birds. Seal the wood with bird-safe sealants to enhance its durability and weather resistance.

4. **Screws and Nails**: Use galvanized screws and nails to assemble your birdhouse. These materials are resistant to rust and corrosion, ensuring a longer life for your creation.

5. **Roofing Materials**: Consider using metal, asphalt, or wooden shingles for the roof, ensuring it is adequately weatherproofed and protects the interior from rain and snow.

Safety First: Designing Predator-proof Houses

Creating a safe environment for birds is of paramount importance when building a birdhouse. Predators can pose a significant threat to nesting birds and their fledglings. Here's how to design a predator-proof birdhouse:

1. **Entrance Hole Size**: Design the entrance hole specific to the bird species you want to attract. Make sure the hole is the appropriate size to prevent larger predators from entering.

2. **Mounting Height**: Install the birdhouse at a height that is difficult for predators to access. A height of at least 5 to 10 feet above the ground is generally a safe choice.

3. **Predator Guards**: Incorporate predator guards around the entrance hole, such as a metal plate or wire mesh, to deter squirrels, snakes, and other potential threats.

4. **Secure Latches and Closures**: Ensure that the birdhouse has secure latches or closures that can be easily accessed by birds but are difficult for predators to manipulate.

Assembly Instructions

Now that you have the materials and safety considerations in place let's delve into the step-by-step assembly instructions for your birdhouse:

1. Cut the wood according to your desired birdhouse design using appropriate saws and tools. Sand the edges and surfaces to remove any roughness.
2. Begin by assembling the walls, floor, and roof panels using screws and nails. Attach the pieces securely, ensuring a snug fit to provide stability.
3. Using a hole saw or spade bit, carefully drill the entrance hole according to the specifications of the bird species you want to attract.
4. Secure the roof onto the assembled walls, ensuring it's sloped to allow water runoff. Attach the roofing material (shingles, metal, or asphalt) for weather protection.
5. If desired, add perches or nesting platforms inside the birdhouse to facilitate the nesting process for the birds.
6. Paint the birdhouse using non-toxic, bird-safe paint. Apply a sealant to protect the wood and enhance its longevity.

Installation and Maintenance

After successfully assembling the birdhouse, it's time to install and maintain it to ensure a welcoming abode for our avian friends:

1. Install the birdhouse in a suitable location, considering the specific needs and preferences of the bird species you aim to attract. Make sure it's secure and predator-proof.
2. Position the birdhouse facing away from prevailing winds and direct sunlight, ensuring a comfortable interior for the birds.
3. Regularly clean the birdhouse, especially after nesting seasons, to maintain a hygienic environment. Remove old nests, debris, and parasites.
4. Inspect the birdhouse before each nesting season to ensure its structural integrity and safety. Make any necessary repairs or touch-ups.
5. If your birdhouse has a feeder or bath, ensure they are kept clean and filled regularly to attract more birds to your garden.

By following these step-by-step instructions and guidelines, you can create a functional and safe birdhouse that will not only enhance your outdoor space but also provide a haven for our beloved feathered companions. Happy birdwatching!

| CHAPTER 2 |

DESIGNING AND CREATING BIRD BATHS: STEP-BY-STEP GUIDE

Creating a bird bath from scratch is a fulfilling DIY project that not only beautifies your outdoor space but also provides a vital source of water for our feathered friends. In this comprehensive guide, we will delve into the intricacies of designing and creating a bird bath step by step. From understanding the significance of water for birds to selecting appropriate materials and tools, assembling the components, and maintaining it, we've got you covered in this journey of craftsmanship.

Bird baths are not just a charming addition to your garden; they serve a crucial purpose in the avian world. Providing a consistent and clean water source is essential for the well-being of birds, aiding in their hydration and hygiene. Furthermore, a bird bath can act as a focal point in your garden, attracting various bird species and adding to the natural beauty of your outdoor space.

In this chapter, we will explore the key steps and considerations involved in designing and creating a bird bath. We'll start by discussing the importance of water for birds, followed by an in-depth look at the materials and tools you'll need for this project. Subsequently, we'll guide you through the assembly process, offering detailed steps to ensure a successful creation. Finally, we'll discuss maintenance and winter care, emphasizing the longevity and functionality of your bird bath.

The Importance of Water

Water is a fundamental requirement for all living beings, and birds are no exception. In the wild, birds rely on various natural sources like lakes, rivers, and puddles for drinking and bathing. When it comes to your garden, providing a reliable and accessible water source through a bird bath can make a significant difference.

Hydration

Birds need water to survive, just like any other creature. Water aids in digestion, circulation, and temperature regulation. During hot weather, birds can easily become dehydrated, which can have serious consequences for their health and ability to function effectively. By placing a bird bath in your garden, you offer a vital water source to help them stay hydrated, especially during scorching summers.

Bathing and Feather Maintenance

Birds also use water to bathe, an activity crucial for their feather health. Bathing helps birds keep their feathers clean, which is essential for their ability to fly, regulate body temperature, and remain buoyant in water. Additionally, bathing helps birds get rid of parasites and excessive oil on their feathers, maintaining their insulating properties.

By incorporating a bird bath into your outdoor space, you provide birds with a space to engage in these essential behaviors, contributing to their overall well-being.

Materials and Tools

Before diving into the assembly process, gathering the necessary materials and tools is vital to ensure a smooth and successful project. Let's take an in-depth look at each item:

Materials:

1. Base or Pedestal:

- *Concrete*: Durable and stable, often used for the base due to its weight and resistance to weather.
- *Stone*: Natural and aesthetically pleasing, available in various colors and textures.
- *Ceramic*: Elegant and versatile, providing a classic look to your bird bath.
- *Metal*: Offers a contemporary touch, is durable and can withstand the elements.

2. Bird Bath Basin:

- *Ceramic*: Traditional and visually appealing, available in various designs and colors.
- *Glass*: Elegant and sometimes decorative, adds a touch of sophistication.
- *Stone*: Natural and blends well with garden surroundings, available in different shapes and sizes.
- *Plastic*: Lightweight and economical, offering various design options.

3. Adhesive:

- Select a waterproof adhesive suitable for the materials you've chosen to securely attach the basin to the base.

4. Decorative Elements:

- *Pebbles, Mosaic Tiles, Glass Gems, or Decorative Stones*: These can enhance the aesthetic appeal of your bird bath, allowing you to customize its appearance.

5. Sealer:

- Choose a sealant appropriate for the materials you've used to protect the surface and ensure durability.

6. Water Pump (optional):

- If you wish to incorporate a circulating water feature, you'll need a small water pump that fits your chosen design.

Tools:

1. Safety Gear:

- *Safety Goggles*: Protect your eyes during cutting, drilling, or any activity that could generate debris.
- *Gloves*: Ensure hand protection, especially when handling materials or using adhesives and sealants.
- *Mask*: Guard against inhaling dust or fumes, particularly when using a sealant.

2. Measuring Tools:

- *Tape Measure*: Essential for accurate measurements during the planning and assembly stages.
- *Ruler*: Helpful for precise measurements and marking.

3. Drill and Bits:

- You'll need a drill and appropriate drill bits for creating holes, if necessary, for the water pump or drainage.

4. Level:

- Ensure your bird bath is level during assembly to prevent any tilting or imbalance.

5. Brushes:

- Use brushes to apply adhesive and sealer effectively and evenly.

6. Screws or Fasteners:

- Have screws or fasteners ready if required for securing parts during assembly.

Assembly Process

With all the necessary materials and tools in place, let's proceed to the step-by-step assembly process to create your bird bath.

Step 1: Design and Planning

Before diving into the practical steps, it's essential to spend time designing and planning your bird bath. Consider the following aspects:

- *Size and Shape*: Determine the size and shape of your bird bath, keeping in mind the available space and the aesthetic you wish to achieve.
- *Style*: Choose a style that complements your garden or outdoor area. It can range from classic and traditional to modern and contemporary.
- *Functional Elements*: Decide if you want to incorporate additional features, such as a fountain, which will require a water pump.

Sketch your design, noting the measurements and materials you intend to use. This blueprint will serve as a guide throughout the project.

Step 2: Prepare the Base and Basin

Prepare the Base:

- If your base is composed of multiple parts, carefully assemble them following the manufacturer's instructions.
- Ensure the base is stable and level on the ground, using a level to verify its position.

Prepare the Basin:

- Clean the basin thoroughly, ensuring it's free of any debris, dust, or dirt. If using a new basin, make sure it's in perfect condition.

Step 3: Attach the Basin to the Base

- Apply a generous amount of waterproof adhesive on the top surface of the base. The adhesive should be compatible with both the base and the basin material.
- Carefully place the basin on top of the adhesive, ensuring it's centered and level.
- Press down gently to secure the basin in place. Use a level to check for evenness, adjusting as needed.
- Allow the adhesive to dry completely, adhering to the recommended drying time specified by the manufacturer.

Step 4: Add Decorative Elements

- If you wish to enhance the visual appeal of your bird bath, now is the time to add decorative elements.
- Apply adhesive to the desired areas on the basin and carefully arrange the pebbles, mosaic tiles, glass gems, or other decorative pieces as per your design.
- Allow the adhesive to dry completely, ensuring the decorative elements are securely attached.

Step 5: Apply a Sealant

- Use an appropriate sealant to coat the entire bird bath, including the basin and any added decorative elements.
- The sealant will provide protection against the weather and increase the longevity of your bird bath.
- Follow the manufacturer's instructions regarding the application and drying time for the sealant.

Step 6: Install a Water Pump (Optional)

- If you've opted for a circulating water feature, carefully follow the manufacturer's instructions for the water pump installation.

- Typically, this involves creating a hole in the basin for the pump's tubing and securing the pump in place within the base.

Step 7: Place and Level the Bird Bath

- Find a suitable location in your garden or backyard to place the bird bath, ensuring it's easily visible to birds and accessible for cleaning and maintenance.
- Use a level to ensure the bird bath is sitting evenly on the ground, making adjustments as needed to achieve a level position.

Step 8: Fill and Test

- Fill the basin with clean water, adjusting the water level according to your design and the needs of the birds.
- If you've installed a water pump, turn it on and adjust the water flow to your liking, ensuring it's not too strong to intimidate the birds.

Now that your bird bath is assembled and in place, you can sit back and enjoy the delightful sight of birds frolicking and bathing in your creation.

Maintenance and Winter Care

While creating a bird bath is a satisfying endeavor, proper maintenance is key to ensure its longevity and functionality. Regular care will keep it attractive and enticing to birds. Here are the essential maintenance steps:

Cleaning

- **Regular Cleaning:** Clean the bird bath regularly, ideally every few days, to prevent the buildup of algae, debris, or bird droppings. Scrub the basin and change the water to keep it fresh and inviting for the birds.
- **Algae Prevention:** To deter algae growth, consider adding a few drops of vinegar or hydrogen peroxide to the water during each refill. Alternatively, a gentle scrub with a mild bleach solution (one-part bleach to nine parts water) can help keep the basin clean.
- **Remove Leaves and Debris:** Remove any leaves, twigs, or other debris that accumulate in the bird bath to maintain a clean and inviting environment.

Winter Care

- **Prevent Freezing:** In colder climates, it's crucial to prevent the water from freezing. Consider investing in a birdbath heater, a simple and effective solution to keep the water from solidifying during winter.

- **Bring the Basin Indoors:** Alternatively, during freezing temperatures, bring the basin indoors to prevent damage from ice formation. You can reintroduce it outside once the temperature rises.
- **Provide Warm Water:** During winter, make an effort to provide warm water for the birds. They will appreciate it, and it can be lifesaving, especially in harsh weather conditions.

Inspect and Repair

- **Periodic Inspection:** Regularly inspect your bird bath for any damages, cracks, or loose parts. Address any issues promptly to maintain the bird bath's functionality and appearance.
- **Repair or Replace:** If you notice any damage or deterioration, repair or replace the affected components. It's essential to keep the bird bath in good condition for the birds to use and enjoy.

Refill and Refresh

- **Regular Refilling:** Keep the bird bath filled with clean water at all times, especially during dry periods. Refresh the water regularly to attract more birds and maintain a hygienic environment.
- **Add Ice in Summer:** During the hot summer months, you can add a few ice cubes to the water to help keep it cool and refreshing for the birds.

Designing and creating a bird bath is not only a creative endeavor but a contribution to the well-being of the avian world. Providing a reliable water source for birds can significantly impact their lives, especially during challenging weather conditions. Additionally, a thoughtfully designed bird bath enhances the aesthetics of your garden, creating a harmonious blend of nature and artistry.

By following the step-by-step guide outlined in this chapter and committing to proper maintenance, you'll craft a bird bath that will not only delight your avian visitors but also stand as a testament to your craftsmanship. Enjoy the beauty and wonder that your bird bath will bring to your garden and the delightful interactions it will facilitate with the charming birds that grace your outdoor space.

CHAPTER 3

CRAFTING FEEDERS FROM RECYCLED MATERIALS: STEP-BY-STEP GUIDE

In this chapter, we will delve into the fascinating world of crafting bird feeders using recycled materials. Upcycling, the practice of repurposing discarded items into something new and useful, forms the core of this chapter. We'll explore a step-by-step guide to upcycling materials, preparing them for use, assembling the feeder, and maintaining it to keep our feathered friends returning to our gardens.

Upcycling Ideas for Feeders

Upcycling is a creative and environmentally conscious way to make use of materials that would otherwise end up in landfills. Let's explore a variety of ideas to upcycle different materials into attractive bird feeders.

Plastic Bottles

Plastic bottles are ubiquitous in our daily lives, making them a readily available material for crafting bird feeders. By upcycling plastic bottles, you can create hanging or platform feeders. The process involves cutting the bottle, adding perches, and creating feeding holes for the seeds.

a. Hanging Feeder

1. Materials:

- Empty plastic bottle (cleaned and dried)
- Scissors
- Marker
- Perches (small twigs or wooden dowels)
- String or wire for hanging

2. Steps: a

1. Clean and dry the plastic bottle thoroughly.
2. Mark and cut openings for the birds to access the food.
3. Attach perches by making small holes below the feeding openings and inserting the perches securely.
4. Create a hole at the top of the bottle for hanging.
5. Fill the bottle with birdseed and hang it in a suitable location.

b. Platform Feeder

1. Materials:

- Cleaned plastic bottle
- Scissors
- Wooden plank
- Screws
- String or wire for hanging

2. Steps:

1. Cut the plastic bottle horizontally, leaving the bottom section with the cap intact.
2. Attach the plastic bottle base to a wooden plank using screws, creating a platform.
3. Make small drainage holes in the plastic for rainwater to escape.
4. Hang the platform feeder securely and fill it with birdseed.

Tin Cans

Tin cans can also be repurposed into charming and functional bird feeders. This simple yet effective idea gives a new lease of life to cans that would otherwise end up in the trash.

a. Classic Tin Can Feeder

1. Materials:

- Cleaned tin can
- Sandpaper
- Paint
- Paintbrushes
- Wire or string for hanging

2. Steps:

1. Clean the tin can thoroughly and remove any sharp edges.
2. Sand the surface to ensure a smooth finish for painting.
3. Paint the can with vibrant colors to make it visually appealing to birds and your garden.
4. Once the paint is dry, punch holes near the base for drainage.
5. Attach a sturdy wire or string for hanging, and fill the can with birdseed.

b. Decorative Tin Can Feeder

1. Materials:

- Cleaned tin can
- Craft paper or fabric scraps
- Glue
- Scissors
- String or wire for hanging

2. Steps:

1. Clean the tin can and remove any sharp edges.
2. Cut the craft paper or fabric scraps into desired shapes and glue them onto the can to create a decorative pattern.
3. Punch holes near the base for drainage.
4. Attach a string or wire for hanging, and fill the can with birdseed.

Milk or Juice Cartons

Milk or juice cartons provide a sturdy structure for crafting unique bird feeders. With a bit of creativity, you can design an attractive feeder that fits the theme of your garden.

a. Carton Bird Feeder

1. Materials:

- Cleaned milk or juice carton
- Craft knife
- Paint
- Brushes
- Twine or wire for hanging

2. Steps:

1. Clean and dry the carton thoroughly.
2. Cut out windows or openings on all sides, leaving space for perches.
3. Paint and decorate the carton according to your preference.
4. Make holes for perches and attach them securely.
5. Attach twine or wire for hanging, and fill the feeder with birdseed.

b. Folded Carton Feeder

1. Materials:

- Cleaned milk or juice carton
- Craft knife
- Ruler
- Paint
- Brushes
- String or wire for hanging

2. Steps:

1. Clean and dry the carton thoroughly.
2. Cut and fold the carton into a feeder shape, allowing space for the feed.
3. Paint and decorate the feeder with an appealing design.
4. Punch holes for perches and attach them securely.
5. Attach string or wire for hanging, and fill the feeder with birdseed.

Wood Scraps

Repurposing wood scraps from previous projects is a great way to create bird feeders that blend seamlessly with your garden's aesthetics. This natural material provides a rustic and charming look to your bird feeders.

a. Rustic Wooden Feeder

1. Materials:

- Wood scraps (cleaned and sanded)
- Screws
- Drill
- String or wire for hanging
- Wood glue (optional)

2. Steps:

1. Clean and sand the wood scraps to remove any rough edges or splinters.
2. Arrange the wood pieces to form the feeder structure and secure them with screws or wood glue.
3. Drill holes for perches and feeding stations.
4. Attach string or wire for hanging, and fill the feeder with birdseed.

b. Log Feeder

1. Materials:

- Small log or branch
- Drill with various-sized bits
- Screws
- String or wire for hanging

2. Steps:

1. Clean the log and ensure its dry.
2. Drill holes of varying sizes into the log for perches and feeding stations.
3. Secure the log with screws to create a stable structure.
4. Attach string or wire for hanging, and fill the feeder with birdseed.

Glass Jars

Glass jars provide an elegant and transparent option for crafting bird feeders. By repurposing glass jars, you can create feeders that allow for easy monitoring of seed levels.

a. Glass Jar Feeder

1. Materials:

- Cleaned glass jar with lid
- Drill
- Perches (small dowels or sticks)
- Wire or string for hanging

2. Steps:

1. Clean and dry the glass jar thoroughly.
2. Drill holes in the jar lid for perches and feeding holes
3. Attach perches securely.
4. Attach wire or string for hanging, and fill the jar with birdseed.

Material Preparation

Now that we have explored several upcycling ideas using different materials let's delve into the crucial step of preparing these materials for crafting our bird feeders.

Cleaning and Sanitizing

Cleaning and sanitizing the selected materials is the first and essential step in preparing them for crafting. Proper cleaning ensures the safety and well-being of the birds that will visit your feeder.

a. Plastic Bottles

1. **Cleaning**: Rinse the plastic bottle with warm water to remove any leftover liquids or residues. b. Use a mild dish soap to clean the interior and exterior of the bottle thoroughly. c. Rinse the bottle again to remove any soap residue.
2. **Sanitizing**: a. Fill the bottle with a mixture of water and vinegar (1:1 ratio). b. Shake the bottle vigorously to ensure the sanitizing mixture reaches all parts. c. Rinse the bottle with clean water and let it dry completely before proceeding to the next steps.

b. Tin Cans

1. **Cleaning**: a. Wash the tin can with warm, soapy water to remove any food remnants or labels. b. Use a sponge or brush to scrub the inside and outside of the can. c. Rinse the can thoroughly to remove all soap residue.
2. **Sanitizing**: Fill the can with boiling water and let it sit for a few minutes. b. Empty the can and let it air dry completely.

c. Milk or Juice Cartons

1. **Cleaning**: a. Rinse the carton with warm water to remove any remaining liquids or residue. b. Use a sponge or cloth to clean the interior and exterior of the carton. c. Rinse the carton thoroughly to remove any soap residue.
2. **Sanitizing**: Fill the carton with a mixture of warm water and a few drops of dish soap. b. Shake the carton to ensure the mixture reaches all parts. c. Rinse the carton with clean water and let it dry completely.

d. Wood Scraps

1. **Cleaning**: a. Brush off any loose dirt, dust, or debris from the wood scraps. b. Wipe the wood pieces with a damp cloth to remove any remaining dirt or grime.
2. **Sanitizing**: a. Spray the wood scraps with a mixture of water and mild dish soap. b. Wipe the wood pieces with a clean, damp cloth to remove the soap residue. c. Allow the wood scraps to air dry completely.

e. Glass Jars

1. **Cleaning**: a. Wash the glass jar and lid with warm, soapy water to remove any food residue or labels. b. Use a brush or sponge to clean the inside and outside of the jar and lid. c. Rinse the jar and lid thoroughly to remove all soap residue.
2. **Sanitizing**: a. Fill the glass jar with boiling water and let it sit for a few minutes. b. Empty the jar and let it air dry completely.

Trimming and Shaping

Once the materials are clean and dry, the next step is to trim and shape them to ensure they are safe and suitable for the birds.

a. Plastic Bottles

1. **Trimming**: a. Inspect the plastic bottle for any sharp edges or protrusions. b. Use scissors to trim away any irregularities and ensure a smooth surface.
2. **Shaping**: a. Determine the desired size and shape of the feeder. b. Mark the areas where openings for feeding and perches will be created. c. Use a craft knife or scissors to carefully cut out the marked areas.

b. Tin Cans

1. **Trimming**: a. Examine the can for sharp edges, particularly around the rim and bottom. b. Use sandpaper to smooth down any rough edges, ensuring they are safe for handling.
2. **Shaping**: a. Decide on the placement of feeding holes and drainage holes. b. Mark the spots and use a nail or drill to create the holes in the can.

c. Milk or Juice Cartons

1. **Trimming**: a. Check for any sharp edges or corners on the carton. b. Use scissors to trim and round the edges, making them safe and smooth.
2. **Shaping**: a. Plan the design and shape of the feeder. b. Cut and fold the carton according to the desired design, ensuring ample space for feeding.

d. Wood Scraps

1. **Trimming**: Inspect the wood scraps for any splinters, rough edges, or protruding nails. b. Use sandpaper to smooth the surfaces and remove any imperfections.
2. **Shaping**: a. Determine the dimensions and design of the feeder. b. Cut and shape the wood scraps using appropriate tools, ensuring they fit together securely.

e. Glass Jars

1. **Trimming**: a. Check the rim of the jar for any chips or sharp edges. b. Use sandpaper to smooth down any rough areas, making it safe for handling.
2. **Shaping**: a. Determine where the feeding holes and perches will be located on the jar lid. b. Mark the spots and use a drill to create the necessary holes.

Drilling and Hole Making

Depending on the type of feeder you are creating, you may need to drill holes for perches, feeding stations, or drainage. Properly sized and positioned holes are crucial to the functionality and safety of the bird feeder.

a. Plastic Bottles

1. **Feeding Holes**: Decide on the location and number of feeding holes based on the size and design of the bottle. b. Use a craft knife or drill to carefully create the holes, ensuring they are large enough for the birds to access the food.

2. **Perch Holes**: a. Determine where the perches will be placed. b. Make small holes just below the feeding openings to insert and secure the perches.

3. **Hanging Hole**: a. Create a hole at the top of the bottle for hanging.

b. Tin Cans

1. **Feeding Holes**: a. Decide on the size and placement of the feeding holes based on the can's size and design. b. Use a nail or drill to carefully create the holes, ensuring they are large enough for birds to access the food.

2. **Drainage Holes**: Punch small holes near the base of the can to allow rainwater to drain out.

c. Milk or Juice Cartons

1. **Feeding Holes**: Determine the size and location of the feeding holes based on the carton's design. b. Use a craft knife or scissors to carefully create the holes, ensuring they are suitable for the birds.

2. **Perch Holes**: Choose spots for perches and make small holes below the feeding openings to insert the perches.

d. Wood Scraps

1. **Feeding Holes**: a. Decide on the size and location of the feeding holes based on the feeder's design. b. Use a drill with appropriate bits to carefully create the holes, ensuring they are suitable for the birds.

2. **Perch Holes**: a. Determine where the perches will be placed and make holes for inserting them securely.

e. Glass Jars

1. **Feeding Holes**: a. Decide on the size and placement of the feeding holes based on the jar's lid size and design. b. Use a drill to carefully create the holes, ensuring they are large enough for birds to access the food.

2. **Perch Holes**: a. Determine the location for perches and make holes just below the feeding openings to insert and secure the perches.

Painting and Decorating

Adding a touch of creativity to your bird feeder not only makes it visually appealing but also allows you to personalize it to suit your garden decor.

a. Plastic Bottles

1. **Choosing Colors**: Select bird-safe, non-toxic paint colors that complement your garden's aesthetic.
2. **Painting**: a. Apply paint evenly to the exterior of the bottle, using brushes or spray paint. b. Allow the paint to dry completely before proceeding.

b. Tin Cans

1. **Choosing Colors**: Select bird-safe, non-toxic paint colors that align with your garden's theme.
2. **Painting**: a. Apply paint evenly to the exterior of the can, using brushes or spray paint. b. Let the paint dry completely before hanging or placing the feeder.

c. Milk or Juice Cartons

1. **Choosing Colors**: Choose paint colors that resonate with your garden's design and color scheme.
2. **Painting**: Apply paint to the exterior of the carton, allowing your creativity to shine through. b. Ensure the paint is dry before adding perches and filling the feeder.

d. Wood Scraps

1. **Choosing Colors**: a. Opt for bird-safe, non-toxic paint or wood stains that enhance the natural look of the wood.
2. **Painting or Staining**: Apply paint or stain evenly to the wood pieces, allowing the natural grain to show through if desired. b. Let the paint or stain dry completely before assembling the feeder.

e. Glass Jars

1. **Choosing Colors**: Choose paint colors that complement the colors in your garden, or opt for a transparent look to showcase the seeds inside.
2. **Decorating**: a. Apply paint to the jar lid, creating an attractive pattern or design. b. Allow the paint to dry before inserting perches and filling the feeder.

Assembling the Feeder

With the materials cleaned, shaped, and decorated, it's time to put all the components together and create a functional and appealing bird feeder.

Attaching Perches

Perches are an essential element of a bird feeder, providing birds with a place to rest while they feed.

a. Plastic Bottles

1. **Perch Placement**: Decide where you want the perches to be located based on the bottle's design. b. Mark the spots just below the feeding holes.
2. **Perch Attachment**: a. Insert the perches into the pre-drilled holes securely. b. Ensure the perches are level and stable, providing a comfortable resting place for birds.

b. Tin Cans

1. **Perch Placement**: Determine the locations for perches, ensuring they are evenly spaced around the can. b. Mark the spots for drilling holes.
2. **Perch Attachment**: a. Insert the perches into the pre-drilled holes securely. b. Ensure the perches are level and stable, providing a comfortable resting place for birds.

c. Milk or Juice Cartons

1. **Perch Placement**: a. Decide where you want the perches to be located based on the carton's design. b. Mark the spots just below the feeding holes.
2. **Perch Attachment**: a. Insert the perches into the pre-drilled holes securely. b. Ensure the perches are level and stable, providing a comfortable resting place for birds.

d. Wood Scraps

1. **Perch Placement**: Determine the locations for perches, ensuring they are evenly spaced on the feeder. b. Mark the spots for drilling holes.
2. **Perch Attachment**: a. Insert the perches into the pre-drilled holes securely. b. Ensure the perches are level and stable, providing a comfortable resting place for birds.

e. Glass Jars

1. **Perch Placement**: Decide where you want the perches to be located based on the jar's design. b. Mark the spots just below the feeding holes.
2. **Perch Attachment**: a. Insert the perches into the pre-drilled holes securely. b. Ensure the perches are level and stable, providing a comfortable resting place for birds.

Creating Feeding Openings

Feeding openings are crucial to allow birds easy access to the food inside the feeder.

a. Plastic Bottles

1. **Creating Feeding Holes**: a. Use a craft knife or scissors to carefully cut out the marked feeding holes. b. Smooth the edges to ensure they are safe and comfortable for the birds.

b. Tin Cans

1. **Creating Feeding Holes**: a. Use a nail or drill to carefully create the feeding holes based on the marked spots. b. Smooth the edges to ensure they are safe and comfortable for the birds.

c. Milk or Juice Cartons

1. **Creating Feeding Holes**: a. Use a craft knife or scissors to carefully cut out the marked feeding holes. b. Smooth the edges to ensure they are safe and comfortable for the birds.

d. Wood Scraps

1. **Creating Feeding Holes**: Use a drill with an appropriate bit to create the feeding holes. b. Smooth the edges to ensure they are safe and comfortable for the birds.

e. Glass Jars

1. **Creating Feeding Holes**: a. Use a drill to carefully create the feeding holes based on the marked spots. b. Smooth the edges to ensure they are safe and comfortable for the birds.

Attaching Hanging Mechanisms

For feeders that will be hung, attaching sturdy hanging mechanisms is essential to ensure they are securely suspended.

a. Plastic Bottles

1. **Hanging Mechanism**: a. Thread a strong string or wire through the hole at the top of the bottle. b. Knot the ends securely to create a loop for hanging.

b. Tin Cans

1. **Hanging Mechanism**: a. Attach a wire or string securely to the can's rim, ensuring it is stable for hanging.

c. Milk or Juice Cartons

1. **Hanging Mechanism**: a. Thread a sturdy string or wire through the top or handle of the carton. b. Knot the ends securely to create a loop for hanging.

d. Wood Scraps

1. **Hanging Mechanism**: a. Attach an eye hook or screw securely to the feeder to hang it securely.

e. Glass Jars

1. **Hanging Mechanism**: a. Thread a strong string or wire through the holes in the jar lid. b. Knot the ends securely to create a loop for hanging.

Filling the Feeder

With the feeder assembled and securely hanging, it's time to fill it with the appropriate birdseed or feed.

a. Choosing Birdseed

2. **Selecting Seed Types**: Choose a mix of birdseeds that is suitable for the local bird population in your area. b. Common seed types include sunflower seeds, millet, cracked corn, and nyjer seeds.

3. **Seasonal Considerations**: Adjust the seed mix based on the season to provide appropriate nutrition for the birds.

b. Filling the Feeder

1. **Pouring the Seed**: Carefully pour the selected birdseed into the feeder through the feeding holes.

2. **Avoid Overfilling**: a. Fill the feeder to an appropriate level, avoiding overfilling to prevent wastage and mess.

Hanging or Placing the Feeder

Positioning the feeder in an optimal location is crucial to attract birds and ensure their safety while feeding.

a. Choosing the Location

1. **Safe Distance**: a. Hang or place the feeder at a safe distance from windows and other potential hazards to avoid bird collisions.

2. **Quiet and Peaceful Spot**: Position the feeder in a quiet and peaceful area of your garden to provide birds with a sense of security.

3. **Accessible Yet Hidden**: a. Ensure the feeder is easily accessible to birds while being somewhat hidden from predators.

b. Hanging Securely

1. **Sturdy Support**: a. Hang the feeder from a sturdy branch or hook that can support the weight of the feeder and visiting birds.

2. **Optimal Height**: a. Hang the feeder at a height that is convenient for birds to access while making it difficult for larger animals to reach.

| CHAPTER 4 |

ENGAGING THE COMMUNITY IN DIY BIRDING PROJECTS

Birdwatching has been a cherished activity for people across generations, inviting them to connect with nature and marvel at the beauty of avian life. As our understanding of the significance of bird conservation grows, engaging the community in DIY birding projects becomes increasingly essential. This chapter emphasizes organizing local workshops, establishing birding clubs and societies, initiating community fundraisers, and fostering collaborative projects with schools, parks, and beyond. By uniting individuals with a shared passion for avian life, these initiatives contribute to the conservation and protection of bird habitats, enriching the community's understanding and appreciation of the natural world.

Organizing Local Workshops

Birdwatching is a popular outdoor hobby that allows participants to closely observe and identify avian species. It provides recreational benefits as well as opportunities to connect with nature and learn about wildlife conservation. However, the gear required to fully engage in birding - such as binoculars, spotting scopes, field guides, and recording equipment - can be prohibitively expensive. This results in birdwatching being less accessible to those with limited incomes. Hosting local workshops that teach community members skills in creating their own DIY birdwatching equipment and resources is an excellent way to foster greater interest and participation in birding. Making gear like binoculars and birdhouses from affordable materials lowers barriers to entry. Custom field guides also allow connection to local species. Well-organized workshops at community centers can provide the hands-on learning required for participants to create their own functional and personalized birding tools.

Planning the Workshops

The first steps in planning effective DIY birding workshops should involve partnering with a local organization to secure an appropriate indoor venue space. Nature centers, Audubon societies, public libraries, schools, and universities may be willing to host for free or low cost. Dates should be set strategically during peak spring and fall migration seasons to tie in with public interest. Promoting the workshops through flyers, social media, email newsletters, and outreach to regional birding groups will maximize attendance. Experienced local birders can be hired as instructors to develop curricula and teach skills like making binoculars, bird feeders/houses, bird call recorders, and customized field guides.

Workshop Logistics

Several logistical considerations will help ensure productive DIY birding workshops. Keeping the workshops small, with around 12 participants, allows for more individualized attention and interaction. Stations can be set up around the room, each with materials and visual guides for completing a particular DIY project. Electronic templates for birding resources add customization. Low-cost and reused supplies should be sourced. Basic tools and safety equipment can be loaned out as needed. A system for registration and payment collection will help with organization. Permissions, waivers of liability, and other legal needs should be addressed.

Workshop Format

The workshop format should balance educational lectures with ample hands-on project time. Starting with an introduction to regional bird species and general birdwatching principles provides helpful context. The majority of time can be spent rotating through stations focused on each DIY project, with step-by-step guidance emphasizing creativity. A concluding Q&A allows clarification on any topics, and providing lists of resources will encourage further learning. Wrapping up with a birdwalk to test new gear and identify species combines learning with recreation.

Workshop Objectives

The primary objective of organizing local workshops is to impart knowledge and practical skills related to DIY birding projects. Participants learn about the importance of creating a bird-friendly environment and understand how their actions can positively impact local bird populations. Educating the community about the role of birdhouses, feeders, and baths in supporting avian life is crucial for encouraging sustainable practices.

Expert Guidance

Local workshops are often conducted by experienced birdwatchers, ornithologists, or conservationists. Their expertise and guidance are instrumental in ensuring participants receive accurate and valuable information. Experts can elucidate the significance of using specific materials, building designs, and strategic placements for birdhouses and other DIY structures.

Fostering Environmental Awareness

Apart from teaching practical skills, local workshops play a vital role in fostering environmental awareness. They highlight the interconnectedness of all living beings and emphasize the importance of maintaining a balanced ecosystem. Through these workshops, attendees gain a deeper appreciation for nature and understand their responsibility towards its preservation.

Birding Clubs and Societies

Establishing birding clubs and societies is a dynamic and impactful way to engage the community in DIY birding projects. These clubs provide a dedicated space for individuals with a shared passion for birds to come together, learn from each other, and contribute to the conservation of local bird populations. Birding clubs offer a sense of belonging, where members can exchange tips, experiences, and knowledge related to avian care and habitat preservation.

Creating a Community Hub

Birding clubs serve as community hubs, facilitating interactions and collaborations among like-minded individuals. They create a space where members can meet regularly to discuss birdwatching experiences, share successful DIY birding projects, and plan collective efforts for bird conservation.

Encouraging Education and Learning

One of the significant advantages of birding clubs is their educational aspect. They often organize seminars, workshops, and guest lectures by experts in ornithology and wildlife conservation. These educational opportunities broaden the knowledge base of members and inspire them to contribute more effectively to DIY birding projects.

Enhancing Conservation Efforts

By bringing together a diverse group of bird enthusiasts, birding clubs amplify the impact of conservation initiatives. Collective efforts enable members to contribute to larger-scale projects, such as creating bird sanctuaries, rehabilitating injured birds, or participating in citizen science programs to monitor bird populations.

Fostering the Next Generation of Bird Enthusiasts

Birding clubs play a crucial role in nurturing the next generation of bird enthusiasts. They often organize youth-oriented programs, engaging children and teenagers in educational activities that instill a love for nature and encourage responsible behavior towards the environment.

Community Fundraisers for Bird Projects

Local communities can help fund important bird research, education, and habitat protection initiatives through creative fundraisers. These events raise both awareness and financial support from residents, businesses, and visitors. Careful planning and partnerships are key to successful community fundraisers benefiting bird conservation.

Planning the Fundraiser

First, identify priority local bird projects in need of funding, such as scientific surveys, nature center exhibits, habitat restoration efforts, etc. Reach out to project leaders about fundraising collaboration. Brainstorm engaging fundraiser themes and activities tied to birds, like contests, festivals, races, craft sales, etc. Form a planning team including community partners like nonprofits, schools, businesses, and parks departments. Secure necessary permits, insurance, and venues. Promote the event through media campaigns, social media, flyers, emails, and calendars. Seek sponsorships and donations from local businesses to support costs.

Event Logistics

Consider hosting during spring or fall migration to draw interest. Provide educational elements like speakers, presentations, and guided bird walks to enrich the experience. Offer fun activities for all ages, such as bird-themed games, crafts, contests, food, and music. Have birding optics and resources on display and available to borrow or purchase. Ensure fundraiser components are staffed, accessible, and adhere to all regulations.

Fundraising Strategies

Have a range of options for attendance donations and activity fees. Offer prizes and giveaways related to birding for participation and contests. Include a raffle with bird-themed prizes from local businesses. Set up a central donation booth and have a digital fundraising page. Enable text-to-give options. Provide donation forms across community partners and have a follow-up mechanism. Ensure financial transparency.

Collaborative Projects: Schools, Parks, and Beyond

Collaborative projects involving schools, parks, and other community spaces play a crucial role in engaging a broader audience in DIY birding projects. Schools, in particular, are influential platforms for educating the younger generation about environmental conservation and fostering a sense of responsibility toward the natural world.

Engaging Schools

Collaborations with schools involve integrating DIY birding projects into the educational curriculum. Lesson plans, interactive workshops, and hands-on activities allow students to learn about birds, their habitats, and the importance of creating bird-friendly environments. Engaging schools cultivate a future generation of environmentally conscious citizens.

Parks as Bird-Friendly Spaces

Collaborative projects with parks entail creating bird-friendly spaces within their premises. These initiatives involve setting up birdhouses, feeders, and baths strategically to provide sanctuaries for local bird species. By enhancing biodiversity within parks, these projects create a balanced ecosystem that benefits both wildlife and visitors.

Community-Wide Collaborations

Collaborations with various community entities, including businesses, non-profit organizations, and local government bodies, are essential for large-scale community projects. These partnerships result in citywide initiatives to create bird-friendly spaces, involving the entire community in activities like planting native vegetation, building birdhouses, and implementing bird-friendly policies.

Impact on Community Unity

Collaborative projects promote community unity and instill a sense of pride in working towards a common goal. When diverse members of the community come together to improve their environment and support local bird populations, it creates a strong bond, fostering a culture of environmental responsibility and sustainability.

CONCLUSION

From enhancing your yard's habitat to identifying species, recording observations, honing photography skills, and crafting DIY birding projects, *The Backyard Birding Bible* equips you with all the knowledge and techniques needed to become an expert birder without leaving your garden. This five-in-one guide has taken you on a comprehensive journey into the dynamic world of backyard birds.

You now have the ability to welcome diverse avian species to your yard by landscaping with their favorite plants and adding enticing water features. This book has taught you how birds find and utilize food, water and shelter sources naturally, as well as how to ethically supplement their needs. With an optimal environment, fantastic birds are sure to thrive in your outdoor space.

Monitoring and documenting backyard birds over time provides insights into their daily patterns and seasonal flux. You've learned both analog and digital tools for comprehensively recording the bird species in your yard. Keeping detailed records of your observations shows you firsthand the intriguing behaviors of wild birds.

One of a birder's most valuable skills is the ability to accurately identify the birds they encounter by sight and sound. This book has equipped you with in-depth knowledge of bird anatomy, field marks, plumage variations, vocalizations, movements, and habitat. Refer frequently to the tips in this book as you progress in mastering bird IDs.

The photography section revealed specialized techniques for capturing stunning bird portraits and action shots. You now understand gear selection, optimal camera settings, effective composition and lighting, focusing strategies, and post-processing options. With practice, you'll be able to photograph the splendor of backyard birds to share with fellow birding enthusiasts.

By the end of this book, you've gained practical hands-on experience building your own birdhouses, feeders, and baths. These projects allow you to directly contribute to making your yard an oasis for local and migrating birds. Use the knowledge from this book to brainstorm new innovations and get others involved.

The backyard birding journey never ends. As the seasons change, continue applying what you've learned here to adapt your approach. Allow your fascination with birds to inspire everyday adventure. The observations you record this year will inform your birding next year. Share your passion with friends, family and neighbors, especially the next generation. If this book has sparked a lifelong interest in feathered wildlife, then its purpose has been fulfilled. Now, go explore your backyard bird paradise!

Made in United States
North Haven, CT
03 April 2024

50853943R00076